FOREVER
RECOGNIZE
OTHERS'
GREATNESS

FOREVER
RECOGNIZE
OTHERS'
GREATNESS

Solution-Focused
Strategies for Satisfied Staff,
High-Performing Teams,
and Healthy Bottom Lines

Sarah McVanel and
Brenda Zalter-Minden

BPS
books

Toronto and New York
www.bpsbooks.com

Published in 2015 by
BPS Books
Toronto and New York
www.bpsbooks.com
A division of Bastian Publishing Services Ltd.

ISBN 978-1-77236-025-7 (paperback)
ISBN 978-1-77236-026-4 (ePDF)
ISBN 978-1- 77236-027-1 (ePUB)

Cataloguing-in-Publication Data available from Library and Archives Canada.

F.R.O.G. FOREVER RECOGNIZE OTHERS' GREATNESS and FROG Design are trademarks of Brenda Zalter-Minden.

Cover and text design: Daniel Crack, Kinetics Design, www.kdbooks.ca

To my children, Simonne (ten) and Justin (twelve),
and husband, Mark (of seventeen years),
three of the greatest teachers on the diversity of greatness
and how it can be found at any age
and in the simplest of moments.

–SARAH McVANEL

To one of my many mentors, Steve de Shazer,
who always knew I had a story to share and a book inside me.
You have continued to inspire me from heaven.
I know that, in your minimalist way, you are
simply smiling and giving me the thumbs-up.

–BRENDA ZALTER-MINDEN

Contents

Acknowledgements

Sarah McVanel:

Mark, Justin, and Simonne, you have been my greatest teachers. Thank you for always reminding me that greatness is fluid, powerful, and purposeful. I can't tell you how much your wholehearted support of my dreams has meant to me. This book would not have been possible without it.

Warm thanks to my parents, who have always had faith in me that I would do great things, no matter what I set my mind to, and for seeing my youthful mistakes as opportunities for me to learn.

Thanks to my sister, Darcey, for journeying with me through childhood and showing me strength of character and mind from an incredibly young age, planting the seed in me that even very young children provide windows to the amazing creatures they will become.

My gratitude, as well, to: those who have taken a chance on me, giving me opportunities in my schooling and work to grow into my potential and beyond my knowledge threshold; Paul, for helping me learn the world of publishing and believing in me from just a simple conversation; Mark and John, for your analysis and interpretation of the data used in this book; Pamela and Kim, for mentorship; and Denise, Sandeep, and Don, for countless hours of editing and sharing ideas about how to make the book better.

Finally, Brenda, I could not have written this book without you. You are my anchor, teacher, mentor, friend, and cheerleader all in one. You live abundance of greatness in its humblest form.

Brenda Zalter-Minden:

Heartfelt thanks to my four adult children and their significant others, who have gifted me with courage (Brittany), playfulness (Jonathan), perseverance (Eric), and acceptance (Jay). You all provide a constant source of pride and love in my life. Your daily support allows me to live truly into Forever Recognizing Others' Greatness.

I would also like to thank:

My husband, Gary, for his love, encouragement, and understanding; keeping me on track with his fastidious editing skills; ensuring that I maintain my writing schedule wherever our travels take us; and daily reminders that I am talented and beautiful.

My mom, Sheila, and dad, Leonard, who instilled positive core values that I cherish to this day. In their own unique ways they have always displayed confidence in me to be my best.

The York Centre, for their inspiration; their commitment to work with one another and to serve their clients by adopting the solution-focused philosophy and FROG approach has shifted their culture to recognize their own and others' greatness every day.

The many other organizations, teams, and colleagues I have worked with who have taught me something new every day about the power of FROG and the ripple effect it has on shaping the culture of their people.

Thorana Nelson, for volunteering solution-focused editorial experience and keeping me fuelled.

My dear friend Dr. Heather Fiske, whose creativity helped shape many of the exercises in this book and who continually showers me with love and praise. Her mentorship and guidance are a beacon I always aspire to.

My other friends, for being in my life, from shopping for frogs when the dollar stores were selling out of them to supporting me with encouragement when I didn't think I could do it.

Esther, a bright and dedicated labour and delivery nurse, for coming up with the acronym FROG, which has shaped the way I live and work.

Lastly, my friend and co-author Sarah McVanel. Without you, I would have long given up putting pen to paper. Meeting you has been a blessing. You have allowed me to truly evolve into the person I am today.

Introduction

Acknowledging the Importance of Recognition

We have written this book to help you explore challenges you may be experiencing, particularly in a work setting, and find viable solutions to make your own and others' work experiences better. We do this through a powerful approach we call FROG™ – Forever Recognize Others' Greatness – demonstrating through evidence and real-life examples how recognition, perhaps better than any other tool, unlocks potential and reinvigorates, motivates, and engages individuals.

How important is recognition in organizational life? Here's an illustration.

It was exactly a year ago when Brenda and her husband decided to take a vacation to visit a dear friend. As Brenda tells the story:

We were travelling the magnificent Cabot Trail, staying at a well-known, picturesque hotel.

One night we chose a small restaurant on the premises for dinner. When we entered, a live country music band was playing, and the place was packed. To get a seat, we had no choice but to join others at their table.

Everyone was extremely joyful and seemed to know one another. I quickly learned they all worked for an insurance brokerage, MacLeod Lorway Insurance, and this was one of their semi-annual recognition weekends away. Because they have nine offices across Nova Scotia, they choose the same beautiful and convenient location each time and ensure that all employees are invited with their families. An employee who was single was encouraged to invite some girlfriends to join her for a girls' weekend away. Games are organized, activities are planned, meals are covered, and hospitality rooms set up for those who prefer to relax and unwind. "There are no seminars or training sessions," one employee told me proudly. "The weekend is about us and spending quality time with our loved ones."

I also learned employees are given their birthday off. On the annual Family Day holiday, the company organizes events for employees and their families. They have been doing this since the province of Ontario instituted the day as a statutory holiday even though the province of Nova Scotia only did so in 2015. The company felt it was too long for the employees to wait for a day off between Christmas and Easter. Perhaps not surprisingly, it has no difficulty retaining employees. In fact, there are rarely any job openings: when people retire or relocate, they tell their friends, and the jobs are filled instantly with the best people.

I was so excited by how well this company handled recognition, I sought out the person responsible. Interestingly, no one was willing to accept the credit, as they recognized one another's greatness naturally. After probing further, I was told, "The COO, Louise King, has been here for forty-two years; you should speak with her."

But Louise said, "You shouldn't be speaking with me. It's the owner and founder of the company, our CEO, Stuart MacLeod, who makes all this happen."

And then Stuart said it was because he had the best people working for him that the company was as great as it was. I demanded to know his secret. He finally relented and said, "When I started this company, I realized that the method to success was quite simple. If you take care of your people, they'll take care of you." He added, "If you recognize the right things, then you don't have to make a fuss about things like long service awards because people want to stay."

Our book shares the successes of organizations large and small that already excel at recognition. We want to help you take the steps to improve your own organization in this way, one conversation and one event at a time.

The Need

There certainly is a need for our approach. In preparation for this book, we worked with Metrics@Work, the Canadian engagement survey company, to analyze their database of a quarter of a million completed surveys. (See also Appendix C.) Through this research, which is substantiated by the literature on engagement and countless Human Resources polls, employees still report that, for the most part, they feel undervalued and disengaged. *Given that talent and intellectual capital have become the greatest source of competitive advantage today, organizations must pay closer attention to how they recognize and value their staff.* Retaining top talent who remain invested in leveraging their talents, passions, and virtues on the job is essential.

In our experience, most organizations miss the mark, leaving dollars on the table and customers dissatisfied. They are missing opportunities to innovate and keep their organization viable. This book offers a new way for individuals, teams, and organizations to humanize their workplaces, one positive intention at a time, creating healthier work environments and bottom lines. It's that simple, yet not easy. It builds the business case for the return on investment that results from a strong recognition culture.

The need is great. Millions of individuals spend more time at work than with their families According to the data, they fall somewhere in the spectrum of apathetic to miserable. Many of these individuals intend to leave. Others are what organizational industrial psychologists call "on the job retired." This amounts to a loss of human potential, stifling of confidence, and dampening of interpersonal relationships. Few of us want to go into work unhappy, and we don't believe anyone shows up to do a bad job. It is therefore up to each one of us to do what is within our power to shift our circumstances so we can bring our best self to work and grow every day.

While this book is aimed at helping leaders, employees, and their organizations, it may also be taken as an aid for individuals – for helping *you* to reconnect with what you do best and providing you with the strategies to bring this forward. Our solution-focused approach shows how you can shift your focus to what *is* working, however small, and to listen for and leverage the talents, passions, and virtues of others. We offer you opportunities to reflect, set goals, track progress, and establish intentions, welcoming you as an equal partner, as the expert in your own life, encouraging you to determine what will work best for you. Similarly, we encourage you to invite your colleagues to join you in this journey, exploring how this will best fit your organization.

Unlike the many business books that focus on what is not working, our solution-focused approach has four major tenets that will help people and their organizations excel:

- Pay attention to what is already working
- Make use of what is possible by leveraging existing strengths and resources
- Imagine best possible scenarios
- Set a strengths-based plan with clearly defined small steps

It is all very well to call for recognition personally and in the workplace, but let's also consider *what* gets recognized. For us, that has to be greatness. Greatness is a dynamic, robust, and empowering human experience that individuals, teams, and organizations can use to notice the potential already present, how it can best be leveraged, and how it can be built on for quality of work life, high-functioning teams, and productivity. In fact, some of the factors most highly linked to that sought-after thing called employee engagement, such as trust in the organization and satisfaction in senior leadership, can be improved through meaningful recognition. The recognition of greatness is a tangible and much-needed element for employees to do their best work and stay loyal to the company. *Recognition that is genuine and specific to the individual or team is fundamental in shifting culture as it creates a sustainable space for trust, engagement, and creativity to flourish.*

Throughout this book, we play with FROG not only as an acronym but also as a metaphor, given the applicability to the workplace of the frog's contribution to ecological wellness, the process of metamorphosis it undergoes, and its connections across living systems.

To facilitate assimilation of the concepts and tools, we encourage you to take some time to reflect on the powerful questions at the beginning of each chapter. Scale yourself, from 10 to 1, regarding where you find yourself in relation to the topic and where you want to be. We circle back to these intentions at the end of chapters, encouraging you to set a new intention in order to translate models, data, reflections, and stories from what you've just read into action most meaningful to you.

Our Best Hope for You

We hope that, through reading this book, you will gain clarity on the greatness we know exists within you, grow in your awareness of the greatness all around you, become motivated to recognize greatness as you observe it, and strengthen your confidence to bring new recognition strategies, reflections, and tools to your teams and organization. We hope you keep this book on your shelf throughout your career, pulling it out from time to time as the situation requires, for inspiration or direction that will spur you to action. *Most of all, we hope you realize you already are what you were always destined to be: great.*

One

The Power of Finding Solutions vs. Solving Problems

Opening Reflection

Consider how people in your workplace handle issues. Are there opportunities to learn and explore possibilities or are there barriers and problems? Recognizing others' greatness is a solution-focused approach. It looks at what is already working and offers a blame-free space for exploring options. How much does your culture support and encourage this? How much would you like it to?

We suspect you already know a lot about a solution-focused approach even if you are not familiar with the terminology. On a scale from 10 to 1, with 10 standing for a wealth of knowledge of the solution-focused approach and 1 being the opposite of that, where are you now?

10	9	8	7	6	5	4	3	2	1

Where would you like to be on the scale? What intention could you set now to help you get closer to your desired goal?

Our approach of FROG – Forever Recognize Others' Greatness – constitutes a major paradigm shift for organizations today. How so? Because it turns the usual management approach of problem-solving on its head, emphasizing the "solving" part, not the "problem" part.

The tendency of most organizations is to believe their success is the result of solving problems. Leaders see their job as helping staff or volunteers fix their issues. This means they can begin to see workers who *aren't* solving problems as problems in and of themselves.

Our approach, in contrast, sees talents, passions, and virtues in all people, even when they may not see these qualities themselves or are not operating from their most resourceful place. Our underlying assumption is that all people are capable of great things. Some exhibit this greatness in small and quiet ways while others are more gregarious. Seeing and honouring greatness in people values work done in the past and provides a platform for something even greater.

Giving the A

In his book *The Art of Possibility*, co-authored with his wife Rosamund Stone Zander, Benjamin Zander, an acclaimed conductor and music professor, writes about "giving people the A." Like most educators, he used to tell students how they could earn an A. One day he decided to begin the school year by telling his students they had already earned one. Their only job, he told them, was to write an essay outlining what they had done to earn their A and then to continue to be talented and motivated students for the duration of the semester. He was astounded by the results. Never had any of his students worked harder. They lived into their potential and more, setting higher goals for themselves than he would have set for them. The students already knew best what they needed to do to progress; his job as an educator was to support them, leveraging the talents, passions, and virtues that had already earned them entrance into their prestigious school.

Giving the A in the workplace involves acknowledging and complimenting team members on a job well done while asking them what they think needs to happen next. The people doing the work know what needs to be done or improved. When we see the best in people, even (or especially) when they may feel they deserve it the least, it makes them feel valued. It fosters a more positive workplace, contributing to more enjoyable workdays for all.

Here's an example we love to share. After being exposed to some training in the solution-focused approach, Joanne, a secretary in the Child and Family Centre in Sudbury, Ontario, decided to do something different. Instead of being frustrated with the children's misbehaviour in the waiting room, she began to acknowledge the children for something they were doing well. She also complimented the parents who were managing their children effectively. This simple change in her actions, giving every child the A, created a ripple effect of calmness in a once chaotic environment. Joanne is now heading up a project with her colleagues to purchase frogs of different shapes and sizes to keep the momentum going.

It comes back to a problem-solving vs. a solution-focused approach. If we believe work is made up of problems that need to be solved, we will tend to see the people we manage as needing to fix problems – or even as causing the problems. In contrast, by using a solution-focused approach, we start with the assumptions that our people want things to be better, that solutions are within their grasp, and that they will seize those solutions when given the opportunity. As this book shows, this approach radically changes interactions between leaders and employees and within the workplace generally. It changes these interactions from managerial exercises to inspiring, collegial conversations.

It is sometimes challenging, given the sheer diversity of workplace situations, for leaders to translate the solution-focused approach into management contexts. The great news is that this approach works in almost every organizational environment; it just takes experimentation. We have assisted leaders who have successfully applied this approach when coaching staff, mentoring colleagues, conducting performance reviews, fostering team development, managing organizational change, training leaders, managing conflict, and providing career guidance. It works in settings from clinical to sales, production, R&D, human resources, and more, and in both not-for-profit and for-profit contexts.

Listen, Select, and Build

In their book *Interviewing for Solutions*, Peter De Jong and Insoo Kim Berg discuss the importance of (1) listening for what someone says; (2) selecting the most useful parts; and (3) building questions based on the useful parts. Let's look at each of these.

Listening

Listening begins from a place of acknowledgement that we all have our own set of values and beliefs and make judgements of others based on those values and beliefs. Solution-focused listening requires us to make a conscious decision to focus on people's strengths, resiliencies, and coping strategies. We listen to tease out what is working well for them in the present, what is happening at work and in their lives when things are going smoothly, and what their preferred future is – what work and life look like when things are as they should be.

Listening begins from a place of respect. It is non-judgemental. We're less concerned about the problems and much more interested in individuals' talents, passions, virtues, coping skills, and resiliencies for generating their own unique solutions.

Respect enables us as listeners to see people as the experts in their own lives. It assumes they want to change and have the necessary strengths and resources to find their own solutions.

Listening solicits details of ordinary daily activities to help people realize what they think is ordinary is actually extraordinary. Exploring details with people concerning how they will be living once the problem is solved is a healthy way to shift the focus from problems to solutions.

When conversations take place is important, too. Holding conversations when what people want is already happening – i.e., focusing on what is already working – is a more powerful platform for change than speaking to them when a problem arises.

Listening is a respectful form of curiosity. It inquires, with empathy and understanding, about strengths, resources, and interests. It therefore is about people in their world vs. solely in their present circumstances. We have to learn to listen differently: to listen for what people are saying is most important to them and how they cope. This kind of listening is the essence of conversations that are co-constructed.

Selecting

Listening long enough to build rapport and ensure the individual feels heard enables the most useful information to be selected. This is very different from the usual approach, which is to listen long enough to identify the problem with the person's performance. Our solution-focused approach is not interested in the origin of the problem. This does not mean we are problem-phobic. Rather, as Insoo Kim Berg advises, we "acknowledge and move on."

Focusing on solutions encourages listening for exceptions; it encourages determining, together, the characteristics of situations in which the problem doesn't exist.

During one of our workshops on solution-focused principles, we asked participants to think of a recent struggle and answer four questions (from David Shaked's book *Strength-Based Lean Six Sigma*):

- *What do you want?*
- *What is already working?*
- *What is possible?*
- *What resources and knowledge are available to you already?*

This is meant to be a conversation of five to ten minutes. The leaders practiced, and then took a break. One manager returned to her office and within three minutes was confronted by a staff member with an issue. The manager decided to put what she had just learned into action. Before the manager got to the fourth question, however, the staff member said, "I know exactly what I need to do – thanks!" Off she went feeling empowered to handle the situation. This immediate positive feedback encouraged the manager to continue playing with the solution-focused approach and questions.

As we listen, we select from a wide variety of comments, words, and phrases. The words we choose to focus on can determine the direction of the conversation.

For example, when we're having a disagreement with someone, she may say something like, *"You never help me when I ask you for assistance."* We can choose to become defensive and debate the issue or focus on the underlying request for help. What do people really need and want from us now? When they feel really resourceful (i.e., not as tired, stressed, or problem-focused), how might they articulate themselves differently? We can also select the word "never," saying something like, *"Never? Can you think of a time I helped you in the way you needed me to?"* This question can shift the conversation to a much more productive place from which solutions may be found.

Ironically, sometimes the selecting process goes better by *not* listening to negative talk, as the following story illustrates.

There once was a group of tiny frogs that arranged a climbing competition. The goal was to reach the top of a very high tower.

A big crowd gathered around the tower to see the race and cheer the contestants on, though no one really believed the frogs would reach the top of the tower.

Heard throughout the race were statements like, "Oh, it's way too difficult"; "They will never make it to the top"; "There's not a chance they will succeed"; and "The tower is way too high."

The frogs began collapsing, one by one, but one refused to give up, climbing higher and higher and finally reaching the top.

All the other frogs wanted to know how this one frog managed to do it. They asked him how he found the strength to succeed and reach his goal.

It turned out that the winning frog was deaf!

If we really want to accomplish something, we can choose not to attend to the noise of negativity and discouraging statements. It can be hard to be positive and present for one another in a fast-paced or unhealthy environment; support within the team goes a long way toward making everyone's day easier, more enjoyable, and more productive.

Building

We've looked at listening and selecting. The third step is to build questions based on what we have heard and the positive things we have selected. It turns out that FROG can stand not only for Forever Recognize Others' Greatness but also for five types of solution-focused questions that flow from the kind of listening we are discussing, questions that are Future-oriented, Relationship-focused, Opportunity-seeking, Greatness-goal-setting, and Solution-scaling.

1. Future-Oriented

These questions offer realistic and manageable next steps to actualize a future that is desired. They do so by recognizing the unique talents, passions, and virtues in people's present, past, and future, an essential step toward encouraging positive expectations and outcomes. The future vision is co-constructed using future-oriented language such as "suppose," "imagine," and "when."

The popular miracle question often fits here, when asked in a relaxing, playful setting. In its traditional form it reads like this: *"Suppose that tonight, while you are sleeping, a miracle happens. As a result of this miracle, all of the problems that have brought you here today are solved. But, because you're sleeping, you don't know the miracle has occurred. What is the first thing you will notice tomorrow that will tell you something is different?"* Maintaining a commitment to looking forward rather than backward is a key enabler in a solution-focused approach. Once again, the more time spent eliciting details about the future without the problem, the more likely the individuals will find their solution.

2. Relationship-Focused

Relationship questions help solidify the future vision. Helping people see themselves through others' eyes gives them a window to their talents, passions, and virtues, which they may be struggling to see or acknowledge in themselves in the moment. For example, we can ask, *"What would others notice when the desired outcome has occurred?"* Sometimes people may not know how to answer for themselves but can do so when asked what their best friend or closest colleague might say their best attributes are.

3. Opportunity-Seeking

The past can be helpful when we help others understand when they have been successful, how they have been resilient, and what coping strategies work best for them. This acknowledges their experience and perspective, building on what already works, which they can pull in to the present. Probing with questions like, *"What are your greatest gifts?"* or *"What value can you add without trying?"* enables individuals to think of a time when there was an exception to the problem. This in turn enables them to focus on how those lessons could help them in the present. These questions help people decide how and when they would like to move forward and whether they're ready to detach from their focus on the problem.

4. Greatness-Goal-Setting

Greatness-goal questions seek creative ways to reach the goal identified in conversation – for example, *"What needs to happen for this conversation to be very useful?"* and *"What talents, passions, and virtues already exist to help you with the overall goal?"* These questions create energy for setting next steps toward action. Defining what success will look like helps individuals celebrate progress and momentum.

5. Solution-Scaling

Scaling questions are multi-purpose, subjective, and measurable – they can measure anything from the day after the miracle, the degree of confidence in reaching a goal, the motivation to experiment with new strategies, and so on.

The roots of this measurement approach are actually in therapy, specifically in therapists' need to find alternatives to the illness-based approaches that dominated the field until the 1970s. The founding solution-focused therapists were looking for a more resourceful approach (perhaps the same way people like Marcus Buckingham in the 1990s wondered if focusing on strengths would leverage better business results than focusing on deficits). These therapists were searching for more concrete strategies to mark progress in the journey to wellness and ways to serve clients that would work better than traditional approaches.

One day American therapist Steve de Shazer asked a client during their second session what was already better than when they first met. The client replied, "I've almost reached 10 already!" De Shazer, curious about the idea of using numbers to mark progress, began to experiment using scaling with his clients. He encouraged them to reflect on and describe their successes in this way. As small as it may seem to us today, it was a significant development in therapy; the use of scaling questions is now a fundamental approach in solution-focused practice.

Scaling questions are relatively easy to use. They are extremely versatile, are client-driven, and are adaptable to a wide range of practitioners – coaches and managers can use them as easily as therapists do. These questions enable people to get curious about what's already working, why things aren't any worse, and how they knew to make that good decision for themselves. Overall, they give people a sense of encouragement even when measurements turn out to be on the lower end of the scale. For example, questions may be framed this way: *"Why aren't things worse?"* Scaling questions also drive action; by setting goals, they foster accountability. Individuals are encouraged to imagine where on the scale they would like to be, what is good enough, and how they will notice a difference once they take their first small step.

Solution-Focused Language

We've just spent some time exploring how to build solution-focused questions. The other side of that coin is figuring out how to ask these questions and how to give feedback – in effect, how to use solution-focused language.

The FROG intention is present when direct compliments are offered, for example, "*I am impressed by...*" or "*Something I am noticing that I want to acknowledge is...*" Indirect compliments enable the individual to reconnect with and remember those talents, passions, and virtues others already know are present. For example, "*What do others say and appreciate about you?*" or "*How did you know it was a good idea to...?*" Self-acknowledgement, which is pivotal to our living into our greatness, is encouraged through questions such as, "*What surprised you in this conversation?*" and "*What will you continue to do that is already working?*"

One day Brenda was walking downstairs from her office when she overheard a receptionist yelling at a patient: "How many times have I told you the clinic you are looking for has moved! I don't have time to take you to the correct place every day. You need to keep the piece of paper and follow the directions!"

Brenda was mortified to see the frail elderly woman trying to keep her balance on her walker in the face of this barrage. She took the client to her clinic and helped her settle in.

She then had a decision to make. She could go back to her meeting and forget what happened – after all, she didn't know this receptionist – or she could report the behaviour to the receptionist's supervisor. We've all taken one or both of these options in various situations. However, both assume that an individual's behaviour is bad, and the second assumes it needs to be formally corrected and fixed.

Brenda took a third option: she gave the receptionist the A by believing she wanted to do to a good job and was in the right role. In essence, she took a solution-focused approach.

Asking the receptionist if she could speak to her in private, she said, "I don't know you and yet can imagine that since you choose to work here for this hospital, you are a caring and compassionate woman. I am sure you didn't mean to yell at that frail elderly woman. Are you okay?"

The receptionist began to cry and apologize for her behaviour. Brenda explored how the receptionist had successfully handled stress in other situations and how she could leverage this the next time. By being heard, the woman was able to reconnect with better coping strategies, and to do so with her dignity intact and a renewed focus on being client-centred.

We believe you already practice a solution-focused approach in certain aspects of your life. We encourage you to reflect on this as you read this book. We provide you with various reflections and exercises to help you get started so you can build on what you're already doing well, think about what is working, and simply add to it.

Closing Reflection

Your Possibilities:
Think about the many possibilities available to you.

- *When you reflect on the listen, select, build approach, what resonates for you and how might this positively influence your interactions?*
- *What will it look like when you build from your own expertise and try something new based on what you have just read?*
- *How will you stay flexible and encourage others to stay flexible when trying something new?*
- *How will you develop and share with others the bold new applications of the solution-focused approach?*

Imagine working for an organization that lived these assumptions. How would it be similar or different from your current experience? In this book, you have the opportunity to influence your organization by practicing recognition on the basis of these solution-focused presuppositions.

Inspiration for **Action**

Problem talk creates problems. Solution talk creates solutions.

–STEVE DE SHAZER

Around here we don't look backwards for very long. We keep moving forward, opening up new doors and doing new things because we are curious...and curiosity keeps leading us down new paths.

–WALT DISNEY

That is a way to see it and there is also another way to see it.

–Insoo Kim Berg

The answers you get depend upon the questions you ask.

–Thomas Kuhn

Every person's map of the world is as unique as their thumbprint. There are no two people alike. No two people who understand the same sentence the same way...so in dealing with people you try not to fit them to your concept of what they should be.

–Milton Erickson

Point at solutions instead of at each other.

–Jeffrey Pfeffer and Bob Sutton

Great things are done by a series of small things brought together.

–Vincent van Gogh

Two

Find Greatness Everywhere:
The Ten Dimensions of Greatness

Opening Reflection

This chapter provides you with a definition of greatness and seeks to inspire you to honour your own greatness, personally and professionally. What difference will understanding the importance of recognizing greatness make for you and others? What will it look like? Suppose you become aware of some of your unnoticed talents, passions, and virtues. How will that be helpful to you?

On a scale of 10 to 1, with 10 standing for **"I have a thorough understanding of what recognizing greatness means"** *and 1 being the opposite of that, where are you now?*

10	9	8	7	6	5	4	3	2	1

Where would you like to be? Imagine you are one step higher. What are you doing differently?

In countless studies and articles, authors implore organizations to pay attention to and leverage their biggest asset: the people who work for them. This asset is also the only one that walks out the door every night. How can organizations be sure top talent will return tomorrow, next week, or next month? To what extent do these individuals walk out feeling energized about how they were able to contribute their best work and add value? To what extent do they leave with a sense of accomplishment? What about your colleagues? What about the people who report to or depend on you?

If we do not ensure that people in our organizations can bring the full breadth of their greatness to work – their talents, passions, and virtues – we seriously risk not only losing them (which we will substantiate and explore in chapter five, "Think FROG on a Big Scale: How to Optimize Organizational Recognition") but also not benefiting from the creativity, resourcefulness, and productivity engaged employees bring.

This is not a "motherhood and apple pie" statement. We are in the midst of a talent shortage that shows no signs of easing until 2030. *This talent shortage means employees can easily leave any workplace that does not give them what they need most: the opportunity to do good work, leverage their greatness, and feel valued for it.* Workplace-trending experts warn that engagement and culture are the top challenges of business today for this very reason. Organizations that can create and sustain cultures where people want to stay set themselves up to thrive in spite of ongoing workforce crises.

All too often in our consulting work we see amazingly talented individuals crying out to be asked for their opinion, listened to, and invited to participate in decision making. Employees tell us, *"Respect is not just being polite; it's caring about me as a person, getting to know me, tapping in to my experience and interests, and doing what you say you're going to do."*

In other words, employees are making a simple request: support me in using my gifts, in doing work I am passionate about, and in doing it in a way that doesn't compromise my values and virtues. What they do not always articulate – until they decide to leave the organization, if even then – is they will keep searching for that place until they can bring their best every day.

We believe making this happen for employees is the secret to humanizing the workplace *and* thriving in business today.

Jumping in to Greatness

Our approach, Forever Recognize Others' Greatness (FROG), is grounded in theory you may be familiar with, including appreciative inquiry, humanistic psychology, the field of coaching, and especially solution-focused philosophy. In a business context, you will probably see linkages to servant leadership, emotional intelligence, and engagement theory, to name a few.

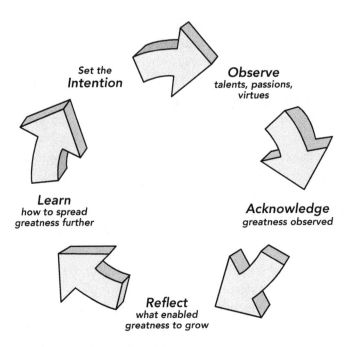

In its most basic form, FROG is about seeing, believing in, and nurturing our own and others' true, most resourceful selves. It's also a process, an ongoing cycle of setting an intention to notice greatness, observe it, acknowledge it, reflect on how it has been able to grow, and learn how to spread it. Put another way:

FROG is the active process of intentionally observing and then acknowledging talents, passions, and virtues so we may reflect and learn how to harness the power of these experiences to grow and evolve them into something bigger.

Let's break this down a little further. There are many important elements in this definition:

- Recognizing others' greatness is an active process. There is no end to looking for greatness and harnessing its power; in fact, if we think we have achieved it, we stop growing
- It is an intentional process. Sometimes we notice greatness by chance. More often it is the result of being more mindful, of intentionally looking for others' true potential
- It requires acknowledgement. Once we observe greatness, we have an obligation to share it with others

- Recognizing greatness means being aware of our own and others':
  - Talents: abilities we were born with and/or have nurtured over time
  - Passions: what makes us jump out of bed in the morning and sparks a light in us
  - Virtues: our innermost values and character that guide who we are
- Recognizing greatness requires us to reflect and learn, to take a step back to understand what is already working, why greatness was able to "show up" in that context, and how to recreate this in other contexts
- Recognizing greatness is a renewable resource, giving us the fuel to do more of what is already working

We begin from the place of intention, formulating for ourselves what leveraging our own and others' greatness will look like. The process, however, is fluid: we can enter it at any point and still have great results. This is the human dimension of the process: engaging in the process of witnessing, acknowledging, and learning from greatness propels us and those around us in the right direction; it builds relationships, improves work performance, and increases satisfaction in what we're doing and the contribution we're making.

Defining Greatness

The dictionary gives two key meanings to greatness: "of large size" and "nobleness of character or eminence." We have some problems with these definitions, for our purposes. "Large" is simplistic, plus what is the cut-off for what is considered large, and is bigger really better? Furthermore, "nobleness of character and eminence" sounds a little old school, doesn't it? Who defines the eminence of someone or something? A king or queen? We believe both definitions fall short of truly capturing the essence of greatness.

Try this definition on for size instead: *Greatness is living our true potential by leveraging our own and others' talents, passions, and virtues.*

The Ten Dimensions of Greatness

Greatness is one of the most dynamic elements of human nature. In our experience, it has ten important dimensions.

1. Scalable

Each person has a wide variety of talents, passions, and virtues and grows into their potential for greatness on their own scale.

Amir was hired to manage a busy but floundering restaurant, inheriting what felt like an army of personnel. His talents included curiosity, optimism, and patience. In his first week he just observed, expecting great efficiency and energy, given the number of staff scheduled. When he observed the opposite, he sat down with each person to ask a simple question: *"Why did you choose to work in service and why here?"*

He learned he had a lot of untapped talent to work with, which required him to realign roles to match gifts.

- Ashley loved working with kids, so she was assigned full-time to the party room
- Gloria was an arts major, so she was delegated to create new aesthetic cocktails for customers and help the tapas chefs present dishes in a visually appealing way
- Rick prided himself on his organizational skills, so he was made the link between the kitchen and wait staff on the busiest evenings
- Tiffany loved working with the public, especially turning bad situations around, so she was given a newly created role of customer-first hostess

Within a few months, energy among staff was buzzing, orders were rarely sent back, more parties were booked, wait lists began to form, and customer complaints decreased. By knowing and leveraging his own gifts, Amir shone a light on the gifts of those who worked for and depended on him.

2. Nurturable

Greatness can be grown, nurtured, and strengthened as people set an intention (such as to leverage the virtue of perseverance), are supported and mentored through the process, and are given an environment that allows greatness to grow. The key here is to believe people are or can be more than they are in that moment. We can support people, from childhood on, to live into their potential at every stage of their life. We do so by helping them focus on what is present in their life when they're at their best.

When Becca worked as a frontline nurse in a busy Emergency Room, she realized she would have to get past her fear of conflict. She had to become more comfortable having tough conversations, delivering bad news about a patient, giving feedback to colleagues about the impact of their behaviour, and suggesting improvements.

Becca's manager coached her through a few initial tough scenarios, and Becca took a few courses. She observed how others handled situations like hers. She practiced different strategies. She tried and failed, and tried and succeeded, as she experimented.

She learned from her successes. Soon her colleagues came to acknowledge her for being able to raise tough issues diplomatically; in fact, they sometimes sought her out for advice.

To this day Becca is amazed how much more comfortable she is when giving challenging feedback. She now formally teaches the skill to other healthcare professionals.

3. Influenceable

Our environment can facilitate the growth of talents, passions, and virtues we may not be consciously aware of in ourselves. We may not see ourselves as a "planner," but that skill may be revealed as we meet challenges, whether a job change, a business opportunity, or having kids. How many of us look back after having children and realize they were our greatest teachers? The experience of having children influences us in ways we could never have planned, as do work, school, leisure pursuits, and other important parts of our life. We have the capability to grow and evolve from what we encounter in our environment.

For as long as he could remember, Larry wanted to be a teacher of young inner city children in the neighbourhood where he grew up. His comfort was in the classroom: he enjoyed seeing the impact of his work on the future of disadvantaged children.

While Larry turned down repeated offers to train to become a principal, he did agree to mentor student teachers. He found himself thriving on the new skills and ideas these teachers brought to the classroom. And he was energized by helping them shift their biases about some of the disadvantaged students who struggle the most. He realized that, by supporting teachers at the very beginning of their careers, he could actually reach tens of thousands of students.

Larry decided to start his Master's degree and then Ph.D. in this field and ended up leaving his elementary school position to teach at a university. His passion made him a gifted and respected researcher, and his talent for teaching made him a top-ranked lecturer, one who always challenged teachers to never write off a student as "broken."

At his retirement party, Larry reflected on his life's work, ending with the statement, "I never would have guessed I would end my career here, but it was clearly what was always meant for me."

4. Non-discriminatory

All people, whether they are young children or older adults, across every lifestyle or life circumstance, have greatness in abundance. Due to the dimensions of scalability, we already know it's most important to focus on each person's level of greatness and the combination of talents, passions, and virtues that are most fundamental. Putting our biases and stereotypes aside enables us to see the greatness in those that society may not expect as much from.

Sharon Gallant grew up in a disadvantaged inner city neighbourhood in a household full of drugs and drug dealers. Her parents were incarcerated when she was fifteen, the family split up, and she went on welfare and soon found herself pregnant. Many of those who knew her didn't believe she could push past the barriers of poverty, sexism, and youth to have a better future.

Fortunately, a few people saw her gifts and potential, when Sharon couldn't even see them herself. She began to listen to their comments and accept them as true. She made the choice to create a better life for herself and her daughter.

Today Sharon is a pro iron man, is in a loving relationship, has a daughter in university, and is the founder of the FAB Foundation, which helps other girls with life experiences similar to hers. She has overcome her disadvantaged socioeconomic past to live into her true greatness, and is recognized the world over for her inspirational work.

5. Identifiable

Any of us can notice greatness in others, even if we're in an environment completely foreign to us. In fact, sometimes that newness allows us to see greatness that others take for granted and no longer notice.

How powerful is it when we can identify elements of greatness in others that they downplay because they come by them so naturally?

Within the first hours of taking on her new assignment mid-year as a new teacher to an energetic class of thirty grade five students, Heather could see the way to manage this rowdy bunch was to help them refocus on what they did best.

- Mohamed, Jetta, and Tomer were quick to tears, so Heather leveraged their sensitivity and empathy by making them peer mediators
- Rory argued a lot about fairness, so she made him the class ombudsman, responsible for working with a few other kids on some "classroom conduct" rules
- Devon seemed not to pay attention, drawing and doodling instead, so Heather had him draw a cartoon while she explained a story or lesson and highlighted the lesson with the class through his drawings

The kids relished their new roles. Some roles were changed and adjusted, but the students found their place in the class on the basis of how they wanted to contribute. Parents, the principal, and other teachers couldn't believe the difference in these kids who happily and productively worked out their own difficulties and accomplished (most of) their schoolwork.

Any time she was asked for her secret, Heather replied, "I just look at what they enjoy and are good at, elevating their potential for greatness. Kids are cool because their gifts are screaming at us if we choose to look and listen."

6. Motivating

The act of acknowledging greatness builds motivation to keep doing what is already working. Often there are many ways to achieve the same end, so why shouldn't people start with what they already have in front of them and go from there, rather than expecting an individual, team, or organization to completely retool?

We have all heard the story of Michael Phelps, the most decorated Olympian in history to date, and we also know that swimming was his outlet to overcome the challenges of ADHD (Attention Deficit Hyperactivity Disorder). Michael, like most kids with ADHD, didn't feel great about himself and struggled in school.

Fortunately, he discovered his gift of swimming early in life, and his mother supported him 110%. He needed structure and consistency, which he had in spades by swimming on a competitive team. The more he accomplished in the pool, the more it built his confidence and gave him strategies he could transfer to other arenas of his life, including school. According to his mother, his ADHD was actually one of the keys to his success.

7. Self-reinforcing

Intentionally noticing and acknowledging greatness makes us that much better at seeing our own and others' greatness. The positive impact to mood, performance, motivation, and relationships compels us to maintain a greatness focus, which, in fact, becomes hard for us to turn off.

Watching the Olympics on TV at her family farm, surrounded by her siblings, Silvia Ruegger decided she would compete as a distance runner one day. She wrote this dream on a piece of paper. When she doubted herself, she read what she had written to remember how far she had come and to keep her focused on where she was going.

Silvia succeeded in going to the 1984 Los Angeles Olympics, finishing an impressive eighth in the women's marathon; to this day she holds the Canadian women's record of 228.36 minutes.

Realizing the power of setting goals through running, she has started the charity Running and Reading for Kids, helping hundreds of young people to be mentored by people who see their greatness.

8. Contagious

Being acknowledged for our greatness in genuine, meaningful ways naturally compels us to pass this positive experience on to others. We begin to process what worked well for us, and to experiment to see whether the same approach will work for others. As we see the positive impact, momentum builds. Over time, acknowledging greatness becomes how we behave and, consequently, defines our culture.

If anyone wants to know what hard work looks like, follow a nurse like Stacy in a busy inpatient unit. Not only was she already one of the hardest working Registered Practical Nurses in the unit, but she also worked those twelve-hour shifts while pregnant.

One day, one of the authors (Sarah) handed her a little squishy frog, explained the FROG acronym, and added, "Stacy, your greatness is your positive attitude and openness to jumping in to a challenge."

Stacy responded with, "Wow, I love this! Can I have some more frogs? I've been wondering how we can start recognizing each other because we have amazing nurses here!"

That's all it took. Sarah delivered a few bags of frogs to her over the course of several months, and every time she saw Stacy, she found that she had given them all away and that she had more ideas for how to spread the culture of recognition, such as "Give me a pat on the back" t-shirts.

9. Inspiring

Acknowledging greatness in others can help them keep the faith if they don't see it in themselves or their environment constrains them. It can be difficult for us to look for greatness in the least-expected places, yet acknowledging it can make a significant difference in someone's life. It can be difficult for us to challenge our assumptions to see greatness where we have never noticed it before. It requires a conscious effort. Greatness is non-discriminatory. No one is off limits to having it.

In a recent workshop, a social worker mentioned she had just started back to work after her maternity leave. She was feeling quite conflicted about being back and doubted she could still make a difference and have a positive impact on her clientele.

Then, out of the blue, a client thanked her at the end of a therapy session for her help, complimenting her for her style and listing the special talents and gifts that had helped her personally.

The compliments reminded the social worker why she had chosen this work in the first place, and she went on to work another twenty years in that program.

10. Life-changing

Simply standing in a place of greatness in our daily life can make a significant difference to how we view ourselves and the world – and can do the same for those whose greatness we acknowledge. Living into our greatness – behaving in a way that leverages our true talents, passions, and virtues – is our best guide to a satisfying and meaningful work and personal life.

Forty-four years ago, when one of the authors (Brenda) was in grade seven, she came to admire and respect a beautiful young teacher named Mrs. Taub. One day she sought advice from her teacher, who welcomed her to join her for lunch.

Mrs. Taub listened as Brenda shared her concerns about a few of the girls from class who were calling her nightly to talk about their problems – from experimentation with drugs to sexual exploits.

Brenda finally paused to ask her teacher to explain what was wrong with her. Why were these students calling her? What came next was the best compliment Brenda had ever received, one that changed and shaped her life forever.

"Brenda, you are such a special young woman. Clearly these students see and trust something in you that allows them to confide in you. You have a maturity and kindness that people can feel and respect. I wouldn't be surprised at all if one day when you are older you become a social worker who helps teens mature and grow through their challenges."

In that very moment Brenda decided she had to do just that, and she never wavered. To this day she wonders if Mrs. Taub realized the lifelong impact she had on a frightened and confused thirteen-year-old girl.

Lessons of Greatness When You Least Expect Them

As parents, we have learned first-hand how important it is to look for the greatness in our children, perhaps digging deep on particularly challenging days. Children never let you forget how important you are to them. They need you to adapt and keep moving toward your best self. You may just be having an "off day," but to them, this may indicate that things aren't on track. When you think you have nothing left to give, they still demand attention from you, whether through colicky nights or tumultuous teen battles. We may not think we elevate ourselves in these moments, but the truth may be quite the contrary.

We often say to ourselves how we *should* be handling things better, comparing ourselves with others who *always* know the right thing to do. Here's the thing: we're always on the journey to being our greatest self, and *sometimes we need to sit in a place of being non-resourceful to figure out the resources we already have within ourselves to draw on and grow.*

By focusing that energy inward, rather than measuring ourselves against external ideals, we invest in searching for our unique blend of talents, passions, and virtues that will provide what we need. After all, if our value as a parent or worker or spouse or leader were in single moments, we would be only a fragment of our true selves. The culmination of our choices and growth is the true picture of who we are. As Anne Morrow Lindbergh put it, *"If you surrender completely to the moments as they pass, you live more richly those moments."*

With almost forty combined years of parental experience now, we look back on how we expected we would be our children's teachers, while in fact, they have been *our* teachers, helping us recognize our greatness and theirs. The same may be said in the professional realm. The challenges we need to overcome in the workplace can teach us more and yield a greater sense of fulfillment than situations where we're able to instinctively use our existing talents. In reality, we often downplay the importance of our contributions because we feel they were "easy" to execute.

What would happen if we saw adversities as opportunities to learn an important lesson that we hadn't yet learned? What if we saw learning those lessons through such experiences as being part of our life agenda? What if we saw our "easy to come by" talents, passions, and virtues as tools for learning these lessons?

In other words, it's about zooming in to see the greatness in the moment, in ourselves, and in others, and then zooming out to see the bigger picture of how the interplay of talents, passions, and virtues paint the most accurate picture of who we and others are and the value we bring.

The great times keep us going. The tough times teach us what we need to learn. The common element through it all is the greatness that is already there, ready to be tapped.

The question is whether we're ready to embrace these moments when greatness shows up in ourselves and others, often when we least expect it. What will we do with these moments? And how can we cultivate this curiosity? One word: intention.

Attending with Intention

We have discussed the importance of intention as it enables us to notice, acknowledge, reflect on, and learn from the greatness all around us. It's true we can notice greatness without an intention to notice it, which again is part of the powerful nature of greatness. It can just "show up" and it's up to us how to respond. Remember, we can set an intention to be more mindful of greatness and to do something with it when we experience it.

Intention is important for so many reasons. Here are just a few:

- We live in a fast-paced world that is full of distractions
- We live part of our life in cyberspace rather than the physical world of human contact
- We grow up from an early age with some strong messages about what true greatness looks like

Over twenty-five years of social psychology research have demonstrated the importance of intentions and their impact on behaviour. Take, for example, Icek Ajzen's theoretical work on planned behaviour. His research was a "game changer" in the world of smoking cessation.

We used to think you needed to raise people's awareness about an undesirable behaviour to impact their choices. However, years and millions of dollars spent on awareness campaigns resulted in little change in smoking habits; in fact, the smoking rates of some groups targeted in these campaigns (such as teenage girls) actually increased. People who wanted to quit, but couldn't, judged themselves as having poor willpower. Professionals working in the field questioned their effectiveness.

Ajzen and colleagues found that the best predictor for determining a behavioural change was not exposure to information but the individual's intention about the behaviour; in other words, whether a person is cognitively ready to do something differently. Intention, he found, is determined by three key things:

1. Attitude toward the behaviour (e.g., Do I want to find this valuable?)

2. Subjective norms (e.g., Do people I care about value this behaviour?)

3. Perceived control over that behaviour (e.g., Do I think I can?)

We can take these valuable insights and apply them to our understanding of people's views about recognizing greatness, starting first with their attitude toward it. For example, do people believe there is value in recognizing others' greatness? Do they believe greatness is accessible to anyone? Or do they believe this is the domain of just a few?

What's with the Attitude?
Think about these questions:
- *In what ways do I already focus on greatness?*
- *In what ways could my workplace benefit from an increased focus on and acknowledgment of people's greatness?*
- *In what ways could my personal relationships benefit from an increased focus on and acknowledgement of people's greatness?*
- *In what ways have I seen recognition happen that inspire people?*
- *What value would an increased recognition of others have on personal and work relationships?*
- *In what ways will I notice that value taking effect?*

Next, we need to understand how much recognizing greatness is valued by the people closest to individuals, which, as we have learned, has a huge impact on attitude. Do people at work believe the corporate culture acknowledges and values each person's uniqueness, or do they think the corporation expects everyone to be carbon copies of an idealized norm?

Here is the final test. Do the individuals involved believe they have any influence in cultivating greatness in others? Do they feel confident their greatness is valued and can make a difference?

The theory of planned behaviour indicates that the more individuals perceive the three important factors to be present, the more likely they will live into the intention of recognizing greatness. Following are a few suggestions for how we can cultivate it further.

1. Focus on What We Have Control Over

Stephen Covey shared this important lesson in his bestselling book *The 7 Habits of Highly Effective People*. By focusing on what we can impact (our circle of influence), we direct our energy more effectively. We're concerned about more things than we can actually impact (our circle of concern). In other words, we need to influence what we can and put the rest to the side for now.

2. Focus on Our Own Attitude

How can we sustain an attitude of curiosity and a feeling of hope about greatness? It starts within us. If we believe greatness is of value, then it is. We begin slowly, one small step and intention at a time. Before we know it, we have helped create a ripple effect of influence on those we care about most, and on it goes.

3. Start with the Converted

We probably have some like-minded people around us, which is why we care about them so much. We can start by sharing the ideas in this chapter (or whole book) with them, discussing and exploring the concepts in our work context. What important thing could we do collectively, even if the group is small at first, to start shifting norms?

4. Strength in Numbers

As recognizing greatness begins to yield good results, we can share with more people what we're trying and why. They will no doubt begin to notice others' greatness naturally.

There really is no downside to bringing an elevated intention to recognizing greatness. It may be a little draining at first, if we're putting a lot out there and not getting much back. However, as soon as we feel deterred or tired, we can go back to our original intention. If our intention is to recognize one thing in someone else every day, we can reflect on the small signs of progress that this intention is fuelling compared with before we set this intention. How is it changing us – our behaviour, affect, motivation – for the better? How is it impacting others?

Getting Out of Your Own Way

Consider these questions about some of the things that get in your way of moving forward.

- Where are you on a scale of 10 to 1, with 10 indicating you're able to recognize all the greatness within you and others and 1 being the opposite of that?
- What would one step higher on the scale look and feel like?
- What is stopping you, and, if you can think of something truly tangible, what in this moment can you do to start breaking down that barrier?
- Ask your most resourceful self how able you are to recognize greatness starting right now. What would that look like?
- What, starting now, will you do to begin your greatness journey?

Brenda began a new job after twenty-three years in the same organization, leaving a secure job just a few years before retirement. She was concerned about having to start all over again, building up her reputation and finding the fulfillment she craved. She decided the best way forward was with intention. She set a goal to ask one solution-focused question or pay one compliment in every conversation with every person she spoke to every single day.

Brenda's approach worked miracles. It took very little time for people to trust her and ask her to work with them and their teams. Before long, she noticed they, too, were beginning to ask what was working and paid compliments to one another more often, which gave her the satisfaction of making a difference which she had been craving for years.

When people are primed to shift to a more positive, humanistic work environment, it doesn't take long for a positive ripple effect to begin.

The Momentum of Greatness

The quantity and quality of the greatness we witness should increase exponentially as we look for it, not because we're enabling more greatness to happen but because it's already around us. For example, let's say it's time for you to buy a new car. You didn't think anyone owned an electric car and decide to be an environmental trendsetter. All of a sudden you're driving around noticing electric cars everywhere you go. Did those drivers all buy one on the same day as you? That is unlikely. You're just more tuned in to this aspect of the busy world around you.

We can't underestimate the fact people are motivated to do more of what is reinforced. A whole field of behavioural psychology has shown us how human beings do more of what they're rewarded for and less of what they're punished for. Rewards don't always come from external sources, however. The satisfaction of doing work we value and the good feeling that arises when we acknowledge the value others are making are evidence of what operational learning theory calls "intrinsic reinforcement." If, instead, we look only at what needs to improve and what is not working, we will experience a de-motivating "intrinsic punishment." By focusing on what is working, we not only role model the benefits of focusing on potential rather than problems but also help shape others' behaviour.

We look for greatness not so someone will be motivated to recognize others more (although that is a fringe benefit). We look for it for the simple fact this is the surest way to humanize the workplace. The more we notice greatness, the more we hone our own greatness. The more room people have for their greatness to expand, the faster and better they will be able to do so, yielding benefits not only for them but also for the organization they work for.

Although we have been referring to the importance of recognizing greatness in every context of our life, it's worth looking at the flipside of this practice. The fact is, the more we attend to greatness in one area of our life, the more likely we are to attend to it in other areas. We focus in this book on work, since that's where many of us spend more waking hours than we do with our families and in fitness, leisure, or spiritual activities. Why shouldn't we make our work the most emotionally and cognitively fulfilling it can be? We all deserve that.

Recognition Is Everyone's Business

Recognizing greatness is not just for leaders to do. Nor do certain professional fields have the monopoly on greatness. People in the caring professions don't need to do it more than those who manufac-ture goods. *Every person, team, and organization will grow into its true potential when greatness is valued, nurtured, and reinforced.*

Acknowledging Your Resources

Perhaps in a journal, or even on the blank pages at the end of this book, record your thoughts on these questions:

- *What greatness have you always had?*
- *When was the last time you saw that greatness? How can you tap in to it again?*
- *What is your greatest fear about confronting what is stopping your greatness from being lived?*
- *What would you do if there were no limits?*
- *What are your choices?*
- *What do you need?*
- *How will you know if you are living into your true potential rather than limitations of that greatness?*

The simple act of asking these questions builds momentum because they come from a resourceful place within us.

Begin with a thought grounded in your personal greatness. As we know, the first step is to focus on our attitude, so give words to this greatness. Determine your first next step to live into that greatness. Who also believes in your greatness so they can help reinforce it? Practice your greatness every day and in all settings so it becomes part of who you are. When people notice it, acknowledge this for yourself. No one got you there but you. Keep this cycle going; we're always evolving into who we were always meant to become.

All people need to feel they contribute value, regardless of culture, industry, gender, age, and so forth. Anyone who wants to live into their greatness more can begin by noticing the greatness of others, and acknowledging it in their own way when they see it.

What Is Culture?

An organization's culture is demonstrated by the behaviour of its members and the meanings they associate with that behaviour. Culture is demonstrated through the organization's values, vision, norms, language, systems, symbols, beliefs, and habits. A good friend of ours says culture is to an organization as personality is to an individual. The only difference is that culture is more adaptable. That said, it takes an average of seven to ten years to evolve a culture for the better or worse. When trying to change culture, buckle down for the long haul and target many dimensions – from values to habits – to put sufficient fuel into the change engine.

No matter what we believe to be true about our organizational culture or how we feel about our job, we can choose to focus on greatness. We love the expression, *"Yesterday is gone. Tomorrow has not yet happened. Today is a gift. That's why it's called the present."* We can always search for what, in the present circumstance, in the current moment, is working well already that could be leveraged further.

Organizations are simply the sum of their parts, most importantly the people who work for them. *Each individual has the power to shape the daily experience of the work environment.* As was noted above, each one of us can help shape the culture in our own way. We will discuss organizational and system change further in chapter five, "Think FROG on a Big Scale: How to Optimize Organizational Recognition," but, for now, we encourage you to reflect on how to make a helpful contribution right away. What is the first next step to contribute to a culture that recognizes greatness? What is the first next step to recognize your own greatness? How can you leverage your own greatness as the foundation for contributing to a greatness culture at work?

One of the most difficult places for us to start is to challenge our assumptions about certain people. Why would we want to recognize the greatness in those who haven't demonstrated they're worth it? One key reason: *everyone has greatness; we just may not be seeing it (or may be ignoring signs of it).* We realize that people don't always want to hear this from us, and sometimes dispute it. True, it may take longer to see it in some colleagues, and there could be a few false starts. Put another way, it may take some work to get past our deeply held negative beliefs about others. Our perception is our reality; however, perception is not necessarily a "truth." (More on this in chapter three, "Start with Yourself: How to Free Your Inner FROG.")

Everyone has greatness. Consider three scenarios:

- Susan complains daily that she doesn't have enough time for her clients. She feels management cares only about the bottom line and resents staying late to get her paperwork done. Seeing her clients grow is the most rewarding part of her job

- Gwen is demanding with her staff, giving short deadlines only to hand the work back covered in red ink with all the changes she wants to see. She is quick to point out when she overhears someone being rude to a customer on the phone, but only once a month at staff meetings acknowledges someone who delivered good customer service

- Jeff has a very casual attitude as a journalist. He arrives at work at different times each day, hands in his stories late, and manages to get assigned all the human-interest stories. He spends a lot of time with people when he interviews them, and then gets all the notoriety when his stories get the most praise from readers. When changes in the office happen, he doesn't fight or vocalize support for colleagues but "goes with the flow"

Let's take some time to see where greatness may be in one of these scenarios, looking for Susan's talents, passions, and virtues.

- Talents: She is focused; what matters most to her are her clients. She is an advocate and assertive. She is thorough and sees a job through to completion

- Passions: She is passionate about providing great service. As a result, her clients are loyal to her and the organization

- Virtues: She values quality; for her, having enough time with clients is key to doing high-quality work.

The non-greatness-oriented eye may see all the negatives. If you were Susan's colleague, it might be easy for you to feel worn down by the complaining and righteousness. Her direct supervisor may already be in discussions with human resources about how to deal with her bad attitude.

What would happen if Susan's colleagues and supervisor saw the complaints as poorly worded requests? Perhaps instead of focusing on Susan's problematic behaviour, they could look for and leverage her unique greatness. How might acknowledging her talents, passions, and virtues impact her behaviour and attitude? How might it shift the focus to address the barriers in her way? How much more open might Susan be to discussing how she can leverage her strengths? Might she begin to put aside negative behaviours that are not serving her? After all, a complaint is merely a poorly worded request. How might Susan more productively and proactively bring up possible solutions to issues because she feels valued? How might this shift in the way people think about her impact them positively?

Look at the two other scenarios, too. What might Gwen and Jeff's talents, passions, and virtues be?

No Limits to Greatness Allowed

It starts with you. Now is the perfect time for you to live into the greatness within you. As Margie Warrell shares in her book *Stop Playing Safe*, "The only way out is through." Face this decision with all the greatness you have within. If you are feeling low in resourcefulness, find those around you who know the greatness you have demonstrated in your life, people who can hold the faith for you when you do not see it in yourself.

We have it in ourselves to leapfrog over barriers to begin or continue on our greatness journey. Acknowledging the resourcefulness within ourselves and those all around us will help us push past doubt, challenges, and fears.

Closing Reflection
Acknowledging Your Own Greatness First
- *What have you done well?*
- *Of this list, what could you do more of?*
- *What will you call it when you do it?*
- *What will this greatness look like?*
- *How many times will you practice it per day?*
- *What will people notice about you?*
- *What positive things will people be saying about you directly or to others?*
- *How will this positively impact your life?*
- *How will this positively impact the lives of others?*
- *How will you celebrate the greatness you have brought to the world?*

This reflection may not be easy. However, even small goals and brief reflections will move you forward; any movement in connection with this intention is worth acknowledging, for the courage and energy it takes to

---

do this. That said, if you're not ready to do this reflection, you can come back to it when you are. It is an ongoing journey, fuelled with compassion, maintained with patience, and driven by hope.

Inspiration for **Action**

Work for a cause, not for applause. Live life to express, not to impress.

–Anonymous

It is more important to be of pure intention than of perfect action.

–Ilyas Kassam

Greatness comes when you create something with your life that is not only bigger than you but outlasts you.

–Robin Sharma

Begin doing what you want to do now. We are not living in eternity. We have only this moment, sparkling like a star in our hand – and melting like a snowflake.

–Francis Bacon

Watch your thoughts; they become words.
Watch your words; they become actions.
Watch your actions; they become habits.
Watch your habits; they become character.
Watch your character; it becomes your destiny.

–Lao Tzu

Life is a preparation for the future; and the best preparation for the future is to live as if there were none.

–Albert Einstein

Three

Start with Yourself:
How to Free Your Inner FROG

Opening Reflection

The goal of this chapter is to help you discover the importance of finding, accepting, and acknowledging your own greatness. Suppose you are able to do this freely and comfortably. What difference will this make for you personally and professionally? How will this help you see and acknowledge the greatness in others around you?

Imagine it is six months from now and you are much more comfortable acknowledging your unique talents, passions, and virtues. What difference does this make for you and others? How does this show up for you?

On a scale of 10 to 1, with 10 standing for **"I am extremely comfortable acknowledging my own unique talents, passions, and virtues"** and 1 being the opposite of that, where are you now?

10	9	8	7	6	5	4	3	2	1

Where would you like to be? Imagine you are one step higher. What are you doing differently?

In many indigenous cultures, the frog has deep cultural roots. We have learned that in *Kwakwaka'wakw* it signifies "connection" and in *Tsimshian* "potential." Connection and potential are both essential to the growth and evolution of every being. In indigenous cultures frogs are also a symbolic bridge between other important elements. The frog is said to represent the connection between land and water; without both, humans and other animals – which humans have always depended on for food and warmth – could not survive.

Living in Two Worlds

Many of us describe ourselves as living in two worlds, our work life and personal life, and the push and pull between them is often experienced as a struggle. We deeply need connections in both contexts. In most cases relationships are central to our personal life, but they're important at work, too. One of the greatest predictors of engagement is having a best friend at work, according to the renowned research agency Gallup, a leader in this field for their exhaustive analyses (for more see Buckingham and Coffman's great book *First, Break all the Rules*). Weak and strained relationships at work take a toll on us, not to mention on our productivity, creativity, and ability to do our best work. In other words, potential is sacrificed. Similarly, not having the opportunity to do work we enjoy and that is valued (by us and others) can actually create tensions in relationships at work, and, inevitably, disengagement. We can learn a lot from the lessons of the frog about the importance of both connection and potential.

Greatness is a manifestation of a healthy balance of connection and potential; the pursuit of greatness is not a solitary sport. By bringing our talents, passions, and virtues to the work we do every day, while supporting others to do the same, we not only live into our potential but also support the team and ultimately the organization to achieve more than would be possible if we were narrowly focused on our own agenda. Just ask Scott Kress.

Kress didn't make it to the top of Mount Everest on his own. In his keynotes and book *Learning in Thin Air*, he describes how some of the other climbing teams, made up of accomplished and athletic climbers, never made it to the top because they focused on their own opinions and strengths. His team and others that succeeded knew the only way up the mountain was together. Each person had a strong goal, without a doubt, and sacrificed a great deal for the opportunity to climb to the highest point on earth. However, team members knew facing the elements would require trusting one another. Through connection, they would reach their fullest potential.

In this chapter, we explore the importance of starting from a place of understanding our own unique talents, passions, and virtues and finding ways to honour them in our daily work. Interestingly, by doing so, we help to unlock the potential of those around us. In future chapters, we explore this ripple effect – that by noticing and acknowledging the greatness in ourselves, we fluidly do so with others. *To get to a place of living into greatness as a team and as an organization, our essential first step is to be clear on, and place value on, what we uniquely contribute as individuals.*

Frogs Don't Mature Overnight

Much like the metamorphosis of a frog from egg to tadpole to frog and various renderings in between, we humans are always evolving. Our potential is nourished through all stages of our development.

As we mentioned in the previous chapter, the market on greatness is not cornered by a select few; at every stage of our lives, each of us demonstrates unique potential and continues to grow. Think about children. Even at age two or three, one child shows empathy by comforting a crying playmate, another expresses himself musically with a natural sense of rhythm, and yet another manages to comfort herself whenever she is sleepy, sad, or missing her guardians. None of these children has taken classes in empathy, music, or mindfulness. They spend much of their day in the same daycare environment with the same teachers. They are even measured on the same "scales" for physical and cognitive development. Yet, *each child's gifts naturally and clearly appear; we just have to look for them.* These gifts can be further nurtured and grown over time, when we honour them.

Children may move away from noticing and developing these natural indicators of their true talents, passions, and virtues as they grow up, trying to live into what they're told they should be, do, or think. This is probably true for all of us. Not all of what we're taught is necessarily poor counsel; quite the contrary: many of us are guided by those with our best interests at heart to help us navigate the world around us. However, these rules, expectations, and belief systems are bigger than we are and do not always align. This can sidetrack us from focusing on who we are in the larger context of our lives.

Even guardians can miss the subtle opportunities to support potential because they're working within their own frame of reference of what *should be*; they, too, have belief systems about what will make a child prosper as well as what will be helpful. Guardians who believe, for example, that academics are more important than music may not notice or create opportunities for a child to develop his natural rhythm and musical talents. This doesn't "turn off" the talent, but layers of judgement come to veil the value of music that this child may not be able to explore again until others encourage musical potential or his desire to tap in to that talent is too strong to ignore any longer.

As children move in to their school years, they learn that others gauge their value against certain arenas of life. For example, coaches gauge their strength and athletic capability and skills and tell them if they're good enough to advance. At each practice, coaches direct them in improving their technique – to jump higher, run faster, breathe better, and throw farther. Many teachers begin their feedback on assignments with *"Good try,"* followed by few words (or a whole paragraph) on what to work on next. (See the feedback Sarah's daughter received, ironically enough, regarding her excitement about her mother's book about greatness.)

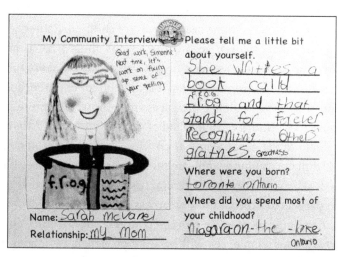

Parents teach children to chew small bites, be more organized, think more seriously about their futures, stop being so silly, and pay more attention. What difference would it make if their *primary focus* from the outset were to acknowledge and recognize their children's talents, passions, and virtues?

Your Roots

Here are a few questions to get you reflecting on the messages you were exposed to, subtly or directly, concerning what was valuable.

- *What talents, passions, and virtues were you praised for (by parents, teachers, others)?*
- *What talents, passions, and virtues did you notice others receiving praise for?*
- *What activities, groups, or interests were valued?*
- *Which activities, groups, or interests were discouraged or even blocked?*
- *How did you overcome roadblocks to following your talents, passions, and virtues?*
- *What seemed to be the definition of a successful life?*

Note that we don't mean to be negative about coaches, teachers, and parents. We have been in all these roles ourselves and know their intentions are almost always in the best interests of children. Rather, we want to emphasize that children absorb the lessons about what is good or bad, superior or inferior, valued or not valued, *at the same time* that they're trying to discover their gifts. It is difficult for children, and even for many adults, to challenge messages from those with more experience, power, or seniority. An implied or explicit message, "*I know what is best, listen to me about who you are and what you need to do differently,*" is difficult to ignore and sometimes bears consequences if it isn't accepted. When an individual's natural talents, passions, and virtues do not run parallel to expectations, greatness can be stifled.

We need guidance, to be sure; it is unrealistic to think children, learners, or new employees will become proficient by relying solely on "instinct." *But the constant focus on telling people where the gaps are rather than exploring where potential already exists means opportunities are missed to reinforce what is working. Supporting individuals to set their own goals and learn for themselves will yield greater success because it aligns with their greatest potential.*

Notice the subtle nuance here. This intention of helping the child, learner, or new employee elevate to their best potential is based on the trust and belief that what is required for them to be great is already present. It involves acknowledging and complimenting existing talents, passions, and virtues by offering guidance and support and sharing knowledge. As was highlighted in chapter one regarding our solution-focused approach, the optimal emphasis is not being the expert in other people's lives; this is often accompanied by ego and power. Rather, it is seeing people as the expert in their own lives; this provides space for people's talents, passions, and virtues to shine.

Being aware of and valuing our own greatness is the grounding we need to be open to receiving knowledge, ideas, and inspiration from others and our environments while having the strength to know when there is a disconnect. If we let others' expectations overshadow our own, we mould ourselves into them, sometimes away from what allows us to be our best.

The Perils of Self-fulfilling Prophecies

There is overwhelming evidence that our expectations impact our behaviours, which in turn impacts outcomes. Sociologist Robert Merton calls this process a self-fulfilling prophecy.

Evan's parents told him he was not smart enough to go to college. He did find some subjects difficult throughout his schooling, which reinforced this belief that he wasn't academically inclined. By high school, he sometimes skipped classes. When he had electives, he chose hands-on tech classes. His guidance counsellors steered him away from university because his grades weren't high enough, and, in any case, Evan told them outright he wasn't planning to go.

While still in school, he had various part-time jobs in the service industry and found he was well liked by co-workers and customers due to his efficiency and personable nature. This led him to pursue hospitality training in college. While he had little interest in the subject, he was confident in his ability to perform in that field.

Within a few years of finishing college, he was bored and unmotivated. Fortunately, along came a girl, who, bound for university, encouraged him to re-examine his beliefs. She didn't know his history as a poor student. What she saw was his thirst for information, ease in solving complex practical problems, and creativity.

Evan did go to university, at twenty-five, and is now a gifted business teacher. He not only helps the academically inclined students but patiently encourages students with negative self-perceptions to examine and see their gifts for what they truly are; he helps every student to see where they will do well in the class. In this environment, he is expected to be a high-performing professional, and he lives into that in a way that aligns his natural talents, passions, and virtues. Evan says he never would have guessed, when he was in high school, he'd end up where he is now. He also says he believes his personal struggles helped make him the teacher he is today.

This story is evidence of Merton's point about self-fulfilling prophecies. Evan's low expectations of himself academically were reflected in his actions, which in turn caused others to expect little from him, reinforcing the original view his parents had that he was not very smart. Later, when his perceptions were challenged and evidence to the contrary presented, Evan put forward much greater effort to prove this new belief to be right. As he did so, he thrived, and a new environment that fit with his greatness allowed him to shine and live up to this new expectation.

This story about the impact of others' assumptions is not an uncommon one. We know many talented professional coaches who had first careers in math, finance, and business because they were told this was valuable and guaranteed success in life. Professional coaching, as a second, third, or even fourth career, resulted from their purposeful search for what would fulfill them professionally and allow them to add the most value.

There was a point when they had to step back and ask, *"If I am successful and good at my job, but not fulfilled, does that mean I should keep doing it?"* Some even asked themselves, *"How did I get to this point in my career with so much schooling and experience in a job I don't even like?"*

These are intelligent, talented people. It goes to show that all of us may be susceptible to behaving in a way that aligns to others' expectations and ignoring our own inner instincts that it is not the right fit.

Part of our metamorphosis is sorting out who we are from what others expect us to be. Probably the best way to describe this is as a journey. *We never reach who we are; we are always becoming.* Greatness, after all, is scalable and nurturable.

The other important point is that momentum is lost when the focus is on *deficits* because less attention is paid to the important details of what is already working. Genuine acknowledgement of *strengths* requires a suspension of the view that a particular model works for all; rather, the subtleties of what is present when individuals are at their best will yield greater gains than trying to change them. *Intentional reflection and a large measure of courage are required for us to reject the noise of external or internalized messages of deficits and examine our greatness.*

What would happen if we were committed to living from a place of greatness rather than deficits? How would that shift our attention, both in how we think of ourselves and how we think about and relate to others? Would a shift in focus enable us to live in a way that is truer to ourselves?

What You Focus on Grows

Sometimes we're surprised, during coaching sessions or when consulting with teams, by how little people are able to acknowledge about themselves. When we ask individuals to list all their strengths, they feel uncomfortable sharing these with others.

Case in point. We teach an exercise we call resource gossiping, which, in a nutshell, is speaking positively about others as if they were not present. This powerful exercise was first taught to Brenda in a workshop offered by Peter Szabó. She has since incorporated it into most of the workshops she delivers. In our work together, we have people, one by one, turn their back to a few colleagues and have the colleagues describe what they most value, appreciate, and respect in that individual. That's right; we force people to listen to examples of all their talents, passions, and virtues. We don't even let them interject and downplay a description of strength. Imagine the cruelty!

So when this exercise is over, do the individuals boo us out of the room? Quite the contrary. In the space of a few minutes, they begin to say things like:

- I feel so good!

- I had no idea how much my colleagues knew about me

- Wow, I wish I could do this every day!
- It was difficult to sit there and listen to all that great stuff, but I needed to hear it
- We need to do this more often in the workplace
- I am going to try this at my next department meeting

That is a great call to action. What if we did take a few minutes on a regular basis to tell our colleagues what was great about them? What if we were able to end each week answering in the affirmative the question, *"Did I let my colleagues know how much I appreciated and needed them this week?"*

What if we used strategies like resource gossiping as a way to kick off new projects or team building?

Sarah recently facilitated a retreat for a group of elementary teachers on their first day back after summer holidays. Even though there were two new teachers who had been with the school for only five hours before the exercise began, by the end of the retreat they were amazed by how much resourceful information they knew about their colleagues and how much their colleagues had already figured out about them. Talk about a powerful way to onboard new people!

What if every time we heard something positive about someone, we passed along what we heard? What if we looked for this in ourselves? Might we become more comfortable hearing nice *true* things being said about us?

What we focus on grows. Why not focus on possibility and potential rather than roadblocks and deficits? When we focus on what we're good at, and what we enjoy and allow ourselves to be energized by these things, we encourage an authentic cultivation of our talents, expediting the trajectory of our greatness.

Yes, we can make some gains by focusing on improvements. We're not suggesting people should ignore their gut or feedback from others about what they could do better. After all, improvement is crucial to living into our potential. However, in our experience, the issue often is that individuals are not honouring their talents, passions, and virtues or their environment does not value or leverage them. The point is, when we focus on what we lack – what *should* be or what we *should* have – it's harder for us to hear the wise inner voice that can show us the path to living into who we truly are when we're at our best.

Keep the Gossip Going

As for those folks who have a positive experience with resource gossiping in a workshop or retreat, do you think they automatically make this practice part of their follow-up meetings and interactions? Unfortunately, often they do not; it's not quite that simple, for a host of reasons, from engrained practices to more deeply rooted messages focused on fixing what's *not* working. (Remember the first chapter of this book, "The Power of Finding Solutions vs. Solving Problems.")

Resource Gossiping...About Ourselves!

Take out a pen and paper. Free-write (without editing or over-thinking your answers) your responses to the prompts below. Set your timer to five minutes for step 1 and another five minutes for step 2.

1. List all your talents, passions, and virtues.

2. Reflect on the following questions and list answers:

- *What compliments do people give you?*
- *What accomplishments are you most proud of?*
- *What altruistic gestures have you made?*
- *What do people admire about you?*

3. Review your responses to both steps. What stands out for you? What resonates most for you? Was this exercise difficult? If you can't resource gossip about yourself, you may struggle to do it for others, so why not push past your discomfort and repeat the exercise again right now?

Try this exercise a few times over the course of a week and see how it gets easier.

We lose energy and momentum when we get sidetracked from consistently focusing on what is working. It is tempting to revert back to how we've always thought or behaved. It is a lot easier to ride the wave of expectations than challenge them (even if they're just in our own contemplations). The hard work has to be done, however, or else we get stuck in that self-fulfilling prophecy, striving to meet others' expectations in place of our own.

Sarah recalls something a friend who was facing a divorce in her early thirties with two small children told her. She said she felt she had been living someone else's life, one that others expected her to live, everything from how much school to take to marrying someone she didn't love to moving houses based on her then-husband's whims to taking jobs people said would be "perfect" for her.

Rewriting Your Life Story of "Failures"*

Think about five "failures" you have experienced. Perhaps they were lessons you had to learn the hard way. Maybe they caused significant distress or maybe they were a "bump in the road" of life. Probably you would be tempted to wish you had never experienced them. List them below.

1.
2.
3.
4.
5.

Now reflect on how these experiences have helped you or served you in some way in your life. How did they teach you something about yourself that you may not have learned otherwise? How did they help you to make a courageous choice? How did they motivate you? How did they help you tap in to your talents, align you to something you were passionate about, or leverage your natural virtues? Note these reflections beside the list of five (individually, or holistically if you see a pattern).

Now think about five past and present successes you have experienced. Possibilities may be when you passed your driving test, graduated from college or university, or got your first job.

1.
2.
3.
4.
5.

Reflect on how you feel remembering these experiences. What does this teach you about yourself? How did you succeed at these things? What talents, passions, and virtues came to the surface for you? Note these reflections beside the list of five (individually, or holistically if you see a pattern).

* Adapted from an exercise created by Sue Young.

Sarah's friend finally took the time and made a difficult choice to start living according to who she was, not what others wanted her to be, which meant she couldn't do so with the person she had married and not even in the city where she was living. Despite the hard work of rebuilding a new life, the alternative to her was worse.

Can you resonate with her in some way? Have you faced a difficult life choice to live by who you are vs. how others want you to be? Keep in mind, we're still making a choice when we do *not* honour who we are.

We believe Sarah's friend demonstrated bravery and wisdom. Conventional ways of thinking may have painted her experience as a failure. We disagree, although we do agree this was a hard way to learn about the importance of honouring our inner wisdom. What came out of this, however, was a mom who could grow again, who was happy, and who was learning to live by what was most important: her innermost truths about who she was and who she needed to be to lead her best life. Not surprisingly, her boys are doing really well.

What if there was no other choice but to do this hard work of living into our greatness? What if we believed the *only* way to lead our best and most fulfilling life was to constantly challenge ourselves (and others) to authentically acknowledge greatness? Let's put that more strongly. What if you felt *you couldn't survive unless you did*? We're not talking physically. Your body could go on, but the true you of who you were always meant to be might never mature, or could even perish.

Frogs Cause Warts and Other Myths

There is a myth in our culture that you can get a wart from touching a frog. If that were the case, our frog-catching boys would have been covered in warts every summer! We know from experience this is a myth. How, then, could this cautionary tale continue to be passed on? We don't even remember where the belief came from.

Isn't this true of so many beliefs? We believe things to be the case even though we can't remember when we first learned them. Even if we could, the person we learned it from had "always known it" so we can't place the origin of the beliefs. Can we even place the origins of harmful workplace beliefs, such as that a colleague or supervisor is incompetent or unethical or mean? How often do we question whether such beliefs are still warranted (or if they ever were)? To the contrary, we're able to see only what reinforces that belief to be true rather than any evidence to the contrary.

This is also true when it comes to the beliefs we have about ourselves. We suffer from what is called confirmation bias, a natural tendency to seek evidence to support what we believe and ignore (not intentionally but automatically) evidence that may challenge our thinking.

Back to our friend Evan, who found ample evidence, every time he struggled in school, that he was not proficient academically. What if his parents and teachers had suggested his struggles were expected and a sign that he was pushing himself? What if that sense of drive were internalized to the point that it was satisfying (intrinsic motivation)? What if, when he worked hard he was rewarded by his parents with praise and compensation for maintaining average to good marks on his report cards (extrinsic motivation)?

A key difference between the two perspectives is whether deficits or strengths are emphasized. We can use our confirmation bias to our advantage rather than letting it pull us away from our talents. Rewriting or adjusting the script of our lives with a focus on greatness allows our self-fulfilling prophecy to work *for* rather than *against* us. Getting to the root of our self-perceptions isn't easy. After all, when did we acquire a belief in the first place? (You may have experienced this difficulty in the exercises above, "Reflecting on Our Roots" and "Rewriting Our Life Story of 'Failures.'") It's astounding how deeply rooted some of our beliefs about ourselves are. *It is worth pushing through to see what exists within ourselves that is enabling our greatness.*

How Beliefs Become Cyclical

We've just seen how easy it is to create stories about ourselves, about our abilities or lack thereof – the trap of the self-fulfilling prophecy. Beliefs about others can become cyclical, as well. Let's look at Lydia's story.

Lydia's Story

Lydia started a new job in a lab. Her mentor, Steph, seemed very nice and helpful. She was keen to show her the ropes, including telling Lydia the people she should avoid. In particular she warned her about Jessica. "That one's mean. Stay away from her or ignore her if you can't avoid her when she's in one of her moods."

Lydia took Steph's advice, speaking little to Jessica, and, sure enough, she felt Jessica's behaviour go from standoffish and brash one minute to ignoring her next.

One day Jessica exploded over a small error Lydia had made, saying if she didn't know what she was doing she should speak up. Lydia began switching shifts so she didn't have to work with Jessica. Jessica found out she didn't want to work with her, and told her close colleagues that she was impossible to work with and unsafe.

Lydia began to look for a new job as she couldn't imagine having to work with someone who was awful to work with and clearly was not going to leave.

What do you notice about this story? Does it resonate at all with you? Can you see where things started to fall apart? If you could give advice to Lydia, Steph, or Jessica, what would it be? What do you think Jessica's side of the story might be?

Jessica's Story

Jessica was tired and overworked, filling extra shifts until a replacement was found. She was the senior member of the team, so she was offended when she was not asked to mentor the newest staff member, Lydia.

Soon she was relieved she wasn't. Lydia rarely asked for clarification, didn't approach her to learn when there were downtimes, and seemed to stick with only a few of the more junior staff members who didn't show a strong work ethic. Lydia's hopes that a new person on the team would help with the workload were dashed, coming to a head the day Jessica missed processing a huge intake of new orders, failing to meet the one-hour results turnaround time.

Instead of accepting responsibility, Lydia walked away. Before she knew it, Lydia was switching shifts, and Jessica heard through the grapevine people were saying she, the most dedicated member of the team, had made life so unbearable for Lydia that Lydia was going to quit.

At that moment Jessica gave up on Lydia, hoping Lydia would find another job quickly so she wouldn't have to waste any more time with someone so childish and unmotivated.

Do you see Jessica, the "mean" person, in the same way? Do you see how this deficit cycle can continue to spiral downwards? Do you resonate at all with this example of feeling so negative or stuck in a pattern of behaviour in a relationship with someone you can't see a way forward? Have you ever considered how this lack of connection may be hurting you and hindering your satisfaction and productivity?

Can you see Lydia or Jessica in yourself?

One of the things going on in this scenario is what psychologists call fundamental attribution error. Personality, character, and the role behaviour plays are emphasized and little attention is paid to situational influences. Jessica was mean. Lydia was unmotivated.

In fact, Lydia was new, nervous, and influenced by her mentor's perceptions. Confirmation bias kicked in, providing her with evidence for the beliefs she was fed by her mentor. These beliefs settled in before Jessica had an opportunity to offer an alternative view. Jessica felt underappreciated and overworked already and was worried about the safety of the work being produced by the team. She believed younger staff had a lax work ethic and didn't take responsibility for their actions, and quickly found evidence to confirm this with Lydia.

This is what is we mean by getting in our own way and becoming a "psychology lesson." How might you rewrite this story so Lydia and Jessica's talents not only would show up but also would be acknowledged early in this new relationship? What if it went something like this?

Lydia and Jessica's New Story

Lydia met her mentor and learned what she could from her. However, she decided she would reserve judgement about a few of the more negative cautions her mentor passed on to her, particularly about people. Lydia made sure she told each new person she worked with that she was new and wanted feedback if they saw her doing anything that didn't meet quality standards. Clearly she was open to learning all aspects of the job.

Jessica saw in Lydia the nervousness she had felt when she started in the field. She reflected on how much she had learned over the last twenty-five years to get where she was. She invited Lydia to observe her when they had rare moments of downtime.

Lydia found Jessica's approach brash but respected that she wanted to learn. She took Jessica up on her offer.

Jessica didn't talk much while she worked, so Lydia pressed her for information and advice. It was tense for both; however, Jessica's responses were important learning for Lydia. In fact, Lydia had to use what she learned from Jessica the next day on a unique specimen and asked Jessica to check over her work. Jessica was annoyed, as she was busy, but she appreciated the quality control check. When Lydia mishandled a rush order later that shift, she went to Jessica right away, admitting she made a mistake and saying she would appreciate help to rectify it quickly.

Jessica was furious; however, she calmed down and apologized, stating she was concerned patients would not get their results in a timely fashion. The two women worked together to process the specimens quickly, and then, before they left for the day, debriefed regarding how to ensure this mistake would not happen again.

Although Jessica and Lydia both realized they had very different styles, and wouldn't be friends, they respected each other's skills and commitment to the work. Jessica shared with others she knew Lydia was trying, and Lydia shared with people in her circle how much she appreciated Jessica's experience and dedication to patients.

In essence, the two women gave each other the A and learned how to be solution builders rather than problem solvers.

Reflect back on frogs and warts. If we believe touching frogs will give us warts, we avoid them and warn others to do the same. What if we tapped in to our curious selves and wondered why someone might believe this to be so? What if we sought information from people who know about frogs, did our own research, and tested the theory before believing it? (What's the worst that could happen? We could get one wart?)

What if we believed there might be greater benefit from touching frogs than avoiding them? What joy might we get from frogs and being in their environment? What might we come to notice and appreciate about frogs that we didn't before? How might we see the connection of this experience to other passions (such as a love of nature)?

We spend so much time focusing on what we should avoid or on what we don't like in ourselves, in others, and in the workplace. What if a fear or worry never came to be? What if all those things were just mythical warts? Is "not being good at math" really a wart, or is it just that math is harder than languages for us? Perhaps it is not necessarily a barrier, but an opportunity to be challenged. In other words, are there other ways to look at a situation that are a good fit with our belief about ourselves and the world? What might we be doing instead?

Suppose we were to learn to change our beliefs about people by focusing more closely on language. Imagine if, whenever we become frustrated, we replaced the word "frustrated" with "fascinated." Isn't it true that the way we behave and the stories we tell when we are fascinated is much more solution-focused than how we behave when we're frustrated?

In Lydia and Jessica's situation, what happened when Lydia accepted without question the information she received about Jessica, vs. the other scenario in which she took more time to discover the truth for herself, from a place of self-awareness and in the broader context of the workplace?

Chris Argyris studied the perplexing phenomenon of people making assumptions in the absence of certain data and coined a term for it: the ladder of inference. Peter Senge writes extensively about this in his book *The Fifth Discipline: The Art and Practice of the Learning Organization*, because of its relevance at individual, team, and system levels. The scary thing is, these self-generating beliefs largely go untested. Whether we consciously decide we want something, or we have simply repressed a particular passion long ago, an opportunity to live into our true potential is missed because we believe:

- Our assumptions are actually truths
- Our truths are obvious
- Our truths are based on solid data and facts (not assumptions and biases)

Of course we have to be selective regarding information from the outside world as we can't possibly attend to everything. Yet we seem to ignore some fact, choosing what we pay attention to. We may have paid attention to the wrong data in the first place. (Think back to that unhelpful advice Lydia was given by her mentor.) It takes work to catch ourselves in an assumption, to examine whether a belief is grounded in facts. It requires us to declare an intention to question what we believe we know, and calls us to be patient as we work through deep-rooted beliefs over time. (Recall the Listen-Build-Select section in chapter one, "The Power of Finding Solutions vs. Solving Problems.")

What is that colloquial saying about "never assume"? Suffice it to say that assumptions are merely things that are accepted to be true but without ample proof. Sometimes these assumptions stifle our greatness. For example, many of us believe we are not creative or artistic, yet we would be hard-pressed to remember when we first developed the belief. Have we really tested the assumption that we're not artistic? Have we tried any mediums of art? Have we taken special training and not improved? Has even one expert definitively stated we have no artistic talent and should focus on something else? And even if we're not exceptionally gifted at it, might trying our hand at it fulfill another passion of ours? Could art be a means to discovering or enhancing another talent?

Brenda's uncle started painting once his wife passed away. He was in his seventies and never thought he was artistic. Suddenly he was looking for something to fill his time and took art classes. Now not only does his artwork hang in family members' homes, but he has won contests for most creativity. His talent has been enhanced, and he has a renewed sense of pride in himself.

Noticing our beliefs and checking our assumptions is a key strategy in the pathway to greatness. What greatness have we been missing all this time? Or, to ask this question in a more solution-focused way, what greatness is already present and just waiting for us to discover?

Nature has much to teach us, including patience. We can't make a tree grow faster than it is able. We can't expedite spring just because we're tired of the snow. A frog can't skip the pollywog phase. In our fast-paced world, where we can access any information at the touch of our smartphone, patience is becoming an art form.

Finding our own greatness and truly owning it is an exercise in patience. As we've just discussed, *we're going to need to sift through a lot of the biases and assumptions we have about ourselves and those around us in order to get a more accurate picture of our greatness.*

Now would be a good time to go back to any exercises you've skipped in this chapter. (It's okay; we're not offended. We knew you might.) It's tough work to weed through assumptions and biases. It takes effort for us to get clear on our roots and make an intentional shift to a view that is more accurate and serve us well. The clearer we get, the better we feel about our contribution to the world and the more value we add.

No Excuses Necessary for Adding Value

One of our favourite stories is about the janitor who worked for NASA. It goes something like this: One day a young President Kennedy was on a tour of NASA. He came across a janitor mopping the floor. The President asked the man about his job. The janitor replied, "I help put a man on the moon."

Talk about clarity of purpose! The janitor knew the daunting task of defying the laws of physics to propel humans into outer space required someone to clean the building. Imagine how much more energy, creativity, and focus he put into his job with this conviction as opposed to, "My job is to clean the floor." Do you have that same clarity of the importance of your role? If you don't, imagine the impact you could have if you did. If you do, how does it enable you to live into your greatness?

You are a part of your organization because you have a very important role to play. Organizations don't have the money to employ people who don't. You were hired for a reason – because of the value you bring. Do you remember what that value is? How do you live into that value every day? Does that value reflect not only your current role but also your part in the intricate puzzle of why your organization exists, whether it is to serve, to heal, to produce, or otherwise?

You're Hired...Again!

Think back to when you were hired for your last job. We recommend free-writing the answers to these questions (i.e., without filtering your first thoughts):

1. Why were you the best pick for the job?
2. What separated you from the other candidates?
3. What have you done in the role that still sets you apart?
4. How do you make your workplace, colleagues' work lives, and your direct supervisor's job better?
5. On a scale of 10 to 1, with 10 being extremely and 1 being the opposite of that, how much are you living into your unique potential every day?

People sometimes think or talk about what they're *not* doing or how they're *not* contributing. We think this is an unfortunate drain of energy and creativity. It directs attention backwards rather than forward. It deflates the energy we need to keep going and builds in excuses for not living into our potential.

Scary thing is, we're often our worst critic. Any of these sound familiar?

- I have so much to learn
- I have fooled them. They'll figure out the real me soon enough
- I'll never be as smart/funny/efficient as s/he is
- No one will ever follow me
- I am not a real leader/expert/professional

Such thoughts are common examples of what is called the impostor syndrome, in which we struggle to internalize our accomplishments and strengths (more on this in chapter seven, "LeapFROG Your Way Through Roadblocks). If we succeed or are admired, we have a good deflection at the ready, from *"I was just at the right place at the right time"* to *"I'm just lucky, I guess"* to *"I must I have them fooled."* Might this be why participants resist the resource gossiping exercise with us? Focusing on our greatness floods our consciousness with counterevidence to our impostor syndrome.

Much like when people were forced to listen to positive things said by their colleagues, what if we were forced to counter negative thoughts with positive or at least neutral ones? Let's try flipping the points noted above:

- I have learned a lot. I'm always learning
- I sometimes question my value, and, overall, I do good work
- My intelligence/humour/efficiency is different from his/hers (and, really, why am I comparing anyway?)
- I lead the way I want to be led, and most of the time my actions hit the mark
- I'm still building my identity and confidence

Getting caught in a downward spiral of self-judgement is unhelpful, to say the least. Definitive negative statements are rarely accurate. Don't believe us? Consider how often such blanket statements are made about other people? Rarely, right? So why do we think them about ourselves? We're fabulously flawed and gifted all at the same time.

Greatness lives between the lines of flaws and perfection. If we were perfect, we would struggle to connect meaningfully to others. If we were only flawed, we wouldn't be able to reach our potential. Somewhere between the flaws and perfection is where potential and connection live.

Humility Is a Virtue, But...

It takes about three seconds for someone to turn a compliment into a self-deprecating reply. Watch for it. It's incredible to witness. Don't believe us? Give a compliment to someone and see what happens. We'll refund the money you paid for this book if, eight times out of ten, the receiver was able or willing to accept the compliment the way it was intended.

Brenda was supporting a manager, Yenna, to facilitate a challenging conversation with her team. Afterward, the manager pulled Brenda aside and said, "Thank you for the work you've done. I really trust you."

Brenda simply replied, "Thanks."

Yenna sensed Brenda didn't truly hear and absorb the compliment, so she repeated it, adding, "I don't trust people easily. I really trust you."

Brenda realized in that moment it was just as important to Yenna that her compliment be heard and accepted as it was for her to give the compliment.

It is Brenda's practice to ask follow-up questions when she receives improvement feedback. It hit her: Why not ask the same kind of questions to reinforce and truly understand a compliment?

Best Compliment Ever*

Think about the best compliment you ever received. Who gave it to you? Where were you? What was it? How did it make you feel? What was it about the compliment that made it the best you have ever received? How did that compliment impact you, short- or long-term? How did it impact the role of compliments in your life, both in giving them and receiving them? When will it be helpful to remember this compliment again?

* Exercise created by Dr. Heather Fiske.

Even the most confident among us can shrug off compliments. We have met only a few who have mastered the art of accepting a compliment without flinching. Notice whether you deflect compliments. If you do, ask yourself whether what is behind your deflection – the feeling that you don't deserve the compliment – is true. Couldn't at least *part* of that compliment be true? What would happen if you lived into that compliment?

Envision Tomorrow as a "Best Me" Day

1. *Go to a place where you can be alone with your thoughts for at least fifteen minutes, without interruptions. Imagine getting up tomorrow morning at your absolute best, with all your talents, passions, and virtues showing up in their most resourceful form. These may be the items you circled in the last exercise, "You're Hired...Again." Walk through your day in your mind.*

2. *Reflect on these questions (you could even write down your answers):*
   - *What would you be doing and saying?*
   - *What choices would you make?*
   - *How would it impact your decisions, behaviour, and demeanour?*
   - *What would your colleagues notice?*
   - *What would your direct supervisor notice?*
   - *What would your clients notice?*
   - *What would people after work notice?*
   - *What would your energy level be like? Your mood? Your motivation?*
   - *And what else?*

3. *Review what came up for you in this exercise. What seemed to stand out the most for you? Write these thoughts down, too.*

4. *Based on what you noticed...*
   - *If this were a request for you to do more of something in your daily work, what would it be?*
   - *What seems to be most important for you to continue?*
   - *What did not come up that is present in your daily work? How could you do less of this?*
   - *Do you have some choices to make based on these reflections?*

One of the most important messages we hope you get from this book is that *your ability to recognize and foster greatness among those around you derives from recognizing your own greatness.* When you reject compliments, downplaying the importance or intention behind them, it breaks a connection with the providers of the feedback. Not only will they be less likely to give you or others a compliment quite as quickly the next time, but you are role-modeling that compliments should be deflected rather than accepted.

We get it. Humility is a virtue. However, so is insight. Seeing past all the flaws, which we all have, to access and acknowledge our true value, is both the journey and the destination. The challenge is that most of us have paid more attention to what we need to improve rather than what is already working for us.

What is your energy level like after this exercise? What are your most valuable insights and aha moments from this visualization? What does it confirm for you? What one intention could you set as a result?

We encourage you to keep coming back to reflections, exercises, and visualizations such as these. Human beings are not static creatures. We grow and evolve. You can build momentum by putting at least one insight into action.

It's true so many of us were brought up to be humble, not brag about ourselves, and not be the centre of attention. Some of us may have even learned early that we need to "know our place." What we're urging here is the very opposite of selfishness, because recognizing your own greatness enables you to recognize others for their greatness.

We have no doubt you are a polite person with good manners, which are important qualities for a successful life. Now, if we may be so bold, we'd like you to push past those convictions and find your greatness voice.

You have it. It's that nagging gut instinct that tells you you're dissatisfied in a particular job, that you do not like the way a colleague is treating you, or that makes you feel tense in a discussion before you even realize it's turning into an argument. We praise this instinct. It is the wisest part of you that knows when the people and environment around you do not fit with who you truly are and how you deserve to be treated. Put another way, *your gut instinct is your finely tuned radar for determining that the balance of connection and potential in your life is off.*

All we ask is that, as you go on the journey of greatness, you acknowledge that you do have a unique combination of talents, passions, and virtues that make you, forgive the cliché, special. Even if you don't believe this, or you're having a hard time accepting this statement, humour us by doing the exercise below. Please keep on reading.

Getting Real About Who You Really Are

1. Write down your responses to the following questions (without filtering).

   - My colleagues have said they admire this about me:
   - When I am at my best, I:
   - When asked about my talents, my best friend would say this about me:
   - I believe I am good at what I do because I contribute:
   - Something I've worked hard to strike the right balance on is the virtue of:

2. Reviewing your written responses to these questions, circle the points you noted that are **most** important to you. In other words, when you do these, you feel most like you and function at your best.

3. What words or phrases that you circled stand out to you? What is important about them?

   Note that this exercise is never finished. We encourage you to come back to it over and over again.

   Just think how effective you would be if your **first** thought about your responses to these questions was what you're best at vs. what you're not so good at. Think about how much people would be drawn to you if you did more of what people admired about you.

Selfish or Selfless?

In made-for-TV dramas, the catalyst inevitably says something like, *"If you can't do it for yourself, do it for me."* It's so incredibly cliché in that context, but when it comes to recognition, that focus on your own greatness allows you to be resourceful enough to see and identify it in others. In other words, it's actually *selfless* to start first with seeing your own greatness and then turn your attention to others.

We have spoken at length in the first two chapters of this book about intention as a key ingredient in acknowledging the value we bring.

This is something to work at over time. The better the results we get by recognizing others, the more we realize it really starts from within us. For it to be a fluid and effortless process, it needs to become a habit. A habit of thinking differently.

In his book *The Power of Habit*, Charles Duhigg illustrates how habits follow a pathway of:

1. Routine
2. Reward
3. Cue (and the cycle continues)

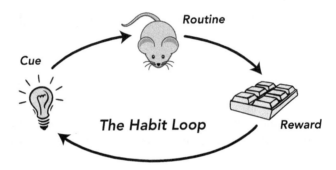

Using this model, we can think about how we can form a habit, or break a habit that is impeding our potential, to recognize greatness in ourselves and others in a more consistent, intentional way.

Habits

Think about the last time you successfully changed a habit. No doubt you will recall the commitment it took to do this. Let's make it easier by starting from a place of reflecting on past successes (and learning from challenges we've run in to) in the formation and breaking of habits.

- *What helped or motivated you to select a habit you wanted to form or change?*
- *When you decided to make this change, what helped you?*
- *If you stumbled along the way, how did those challenges show up to serve you?*
- *What ultimately made you successful?*
- *How did you define success?*

Maybe a habit we realize we needed to break is being unable to accept and internalize a compliment. The cycle might go like this:

1. I deflect a compliment (Routine)

2. I feel virtuous (Reward)

3. The compliment is reiterated again to me (Cue)

Can you see how, without change, this cycle will continue and never allow the true intention of fuelling your greatness to set in? What if you decided to try to alter the habit?

In his research, Duhigg shares that habits can be broken by experimenting with different rewards and cues. Maybe you could experiment with different outlooks: positive, energetic, curious. Do any of these feel like a greater reward than feeling virtuous? Understanding the cues can be tricky.

As we've already explored in this chapter, we have become accustomed to carrying around deep-rooted and often long-established beliefs. However, reflecting on things like where we are when a compliment occurs, who is giving it, what our emotional state is, and so forth, can help us understand what is cueing the need to deflect the compliment and create the reward of feeling virtuous. Then, when we see this cue, we can purposefully try to execute our new routine, and experience a new reward.

Starting from the "cue," we might realize the loop goes something like this:

3. I am surprised by a compliment (Cue)

1. I simply say, *"Thank you"* (Routine)

2. I feel accepted (Reward)

Ah, the realization! By breaking our habit of deflecting compliments, we actually build strong connections with others. This new habit cycle slowly extinguishes our deflection behaviours because we're less surprised the more we hear them and associate them with the positive feeling of being accepted.

Breaking a habit isn't simple or quick, but it's worth the effort if it helps to clear what stands in our way of reaching our potential. As Louis Pasteur said, *"Chance favours the prepared mind."* We can prepare our mind, therefore, to welcome a compliment by seeing such comments as courageous, kind, generous, and, overall, helpful.

Do you have a prepared mind? Do you believe you work in an environment brimming with moments of greatness? If you're not sold (and even if you are), we encourage you to try the exercise below.

Where Is Greatness Hiding?

For a set period of time, maybe a day, maybe a week, make a clear intention to look for examples of greatness, however small, over the course of your day. Don't do anything different from what you normally do. Go to the same meetings, speak with the same people, do the same work. The purpose is to see if the act of noticing allows you to see the talent, passions, and virtues of your colleagues and clients that have been there all along. For "bonus marks," when noticing, why not acknowledge what you see? Oh, and double bonus marks for noticing these things in yourself along the way.

If you look for them, you will see windows of greatness from small to large. Each and every one of these moments is an opportunity to recognize others, in turn reinforcing the behaviour and making it more likely that those individuals will do more of it in the future. The alternative, to ignore the good and see only the bad, is not only to other people's detriment but to yours, as well. You will lose the opportunity to get the best from your colleagues, and, more broadly, the projects they work on and their contribution overall will be of poorer quality.

Here's an example from our experience.

Francine was reassigned to a new team when her job was made redundant. Her soon-to-be ex boss ladled out heavy warnings to her new supervisor that Francine was difficult to work with and was a black sheep who wanted to work only on projects that interested her. Given that the new role required Francine to teach, coach, and mentor others, these qualities, if true, would make her a liability.

Her new supervisor clarified expectations with Francine. He asked her to create a learning plan, paired her with an experienced staff member, and gave her a transition coach to work with.

Far from being a disaster, Francine thrived under these clear expectations. She appreciated any guidance offered to her, displayed a strong willingness to learn, came in early and stayed late, and bent over backwards for her clients. She also found she was happier than at any time in her work. She viewed the redundancy as one of the most positive events in her career. She is still in the role today and continues to grow.

In her previous role, Francine's talents were not truly valued as her boss was looking for deficits, not strengths. She wasn't asked what she needed to be successful or how she could contribute the most value. Although Francine had been doing a job she was very good at, the environment did not allow her to leverage her full gifts. As a result, she had less energy and creativity to offer.

Making the Choice

What you choose becomes who you are. Your choices are your actions, and your actions are the visible evidence to the outside world of those choices.

Taking steps forward, no matter how small, reinforces your commitment to yourself to be who you are supposed to be. Consistently choosing to be who you truly are, rather than what you think others expect you to be, allows you to stay on the path to your own greatness, leveraging both potential and connection. In the end, you'll actually contribute *more* to others by following your greatness path.

Closing Reflection
Daily Greatness Questions
For a day, a week, or a month – you choose the parameters of your inner searching – consider these questions:

- *Have I challenged myself to move beyond what I was capable of yesterday?*
- *Have I been able to do some work today that I'm most passionate about?*
- *Have I offered solutions to problems rather than ignored or complained about them?*
- *Have I honoured my potential by expecting enough of myself (but not too much)?*

- Did I build others up and give them the credit (to their face or when they weren't there)?
- Did I do what was most important first?
- What was my biggest success today, and what did I learn from it?
- Did I do what I said I would do, keeping a promise or fulfilling an expectation?
- Was I my most authentic self today?
- Have I identified how I will recharge so I am ready for more greatness tomorrow?

Inspiration for **Action**

Every child is an artist. The problem is how to remain an artist once we grow up.

–PABLO PICASSO

I can live two months on one good compliment.

–MARK TWAIN

We are prepared for insults, but compliments leave us baffled.

–MASON COOLEY

As we grow up, we adopt negative beliefs and false assumptions and sabotaging fears for the world around us.

–ROBIN SHARMA

The greatest discovery of my generation is that a human being can alter his [her] life by altering his [her] attitude.

–WILLIAM JAMES

Even a small star shines in the darkness.

–FINNISH PROVERB

One cannot teach anybody anything. One can only make them think.

–SOCRATES

Maturity includes the recognition that no one is going to see anything in us that we don't see in ourselves. Stop waiting for a producer. Produce yourself.

–MARIANNE WILLIAMSON

Four

Enable Greatness with Healthy Team Ecosystems

Opening Reflection

The goal of this chapter is to reinforce your understanding of the key ingredients necessary for a healthy team's ecosystem. What five words do you feel best describe a healthy team? What five words best describe your current team? Which are similar and which are different? How many of those aspects of the present team are positive? What untapped opportunities may there be?

On a scale of 10 to 1, with 10 standing for **"I am extremely confident my team's ecosystem is healthy"** and 1 being the opposite of that, where are you now?

10	9	8	7	6	5	4	3	2	1

Where would you like to be? Imagine you are one step higher, what would be different? What one small thing is within the control of the team to try something new? How might success be celebrated so gains could be acknowledged, appreciated, and remembered as other steps are tried?

What do you need to get out of this chapter to provide even greater clarity regarding your team?

When Sarah was looking for a cottage to buy, her realtor said the fastest way to gauge the health of the lake and soil was to look for an abundance of frogs. Because frogs' skin is so sensitive, they cannot sustain the toxicity of an unhealthy ecosystem.

The same can be said for teams. So many factors go into making them healthy, hence the focus of engagement surveys on so many dimensions of satisfaction in the workplace. Recognition is a fundamental variable in this equation, as we will illustrate with the use of data in chapter five. For our purposes here, we will demonstrate that, where there is an abundance of recognition, there is a healthy team ecosystem.

The intention to maintain a healthy environment requires constant nurturing. As organizational development professionals, we have had the good fortune of studying teams for what is working and helping them pass on their greatness to others. We have also spent years working with teams that have neglected their ecosystem and have given up hope they'll ever be healthy enough to thrive.

Sometimes individuals choose another pond. As discussed at the beginning of this book, the tendency of people to leave an unhealthy work environment is only going to grow, given the current shortage of talent. Some, however, will stay, leaping forward by reinvesting in the team and its members. If you are considering taking the leap, reflect first on what a healthy team ecosystem looks like for you and whether you can get there in your current team with some investment. The example used throughout this chapter is a true story of a team that chose to do just that, with huge gains to show for it.

Part 1 of Our Story

When we first started working with this team, it had the lowest engagement scores across the whole healthcare organization. The fifteen staff members had lost hope that their ideas were worth sharing. They did not feel valued and, in some cases, could not stand being in the same room with one another.

We shouldn't have been surprised. They were a pivotal department in the delivery of safe patient care, but as a support department they didn't get any of the credit for the great outcomes they contributed to. They rarely ever heard what went right, but heard loud and clear – sometimes through yelling, accusations, and finger pointing – anything that went wrong.

This team worked in the windowless basement, which was too small and felt disorganized. Their work, most of it requiring them to be on their feet, was fatiguing, especially when their breaks were delayed to address a crisis. Their identities were stripped because they wore a standard uniform, hairnets, and gloves. Unique personalities were seen as a problem rather than a gift. Lack of standardized processes meant people did things differently, frustrating some and leaving others believing people didn't care. They rarely saw anyone but fellow team members, and even then often worked in isolation on task-based work. To top it off, there were communication breakdowns between staff and their supervisor.

By the next survey, over two years later, this team became the most improved in their self-reported engagement scores, going from an average score of under 35% to over 70%. Yet, some things were still the same: they worked in the same space, wore the same uniform, and worked with most of the same staff. So what changed?

Making the Commitment

The very first step in building a healthy team ecosystem is really quite simple. It starts with encouraging people to speak up about what they see as working and what they know is not. *Teams need to be acknowledged for their successes and strengths.* They gain validation when they see people are paying attention and are willing to support them to get back on track. When the team members themselves have faith they'll be a high-functioning team again, a seed of hope is planted, giving them sustenance to begin the journey.

Part 2 of Our Story

Clearly the team was feeling broken. Brenda, the organizational development consultant responsible for working with them, knew trust would need to be earned. When this department's recognition week came around, she asked them how they would like to be recognized.

They were quite surprised with the question initially, then, once they realized she was truly listening, they came up with great ideas. Predominantly they wanted to do something as a team for about fifteen minutes during work hours.

Based on an exercise she'd read about, Brenda bought a box of chocolates and wrapped it in many layers of paper, putting a compliment on each layer – for example, *"Give this gift to someone who smiled at you today,"* or *"Give this gift to someone you trust."*

When Brenda returned for the first fifteen-minute meeting, she presented the gift and the instructions. Each team member was to pass the gift to a member who fit the compliment they uncovered. This continued until everyone had received a special message. The bonus was they shared the chocolates, some laughs, and hope.

They also enjoyed other events they identified as important. More on this later.

There is an adage from continuous quality improvement circles that 80% of issues are process-related and only 20% people-related. This means building a healthy team ecosystem is not about fixing the people. *Looking for examples of when a problem doesn't exist, studying it, and focusing on the exception to the problem can contribute some much-needed positive energy in to team discussions.* A slow but pervasive ripple effect results, making it easier for the team to see the greatness they already possess.

Listening Differently

Once people have begun the journey of noticing greatness in themselves and others, they need to acknowledge their concerns, worries, and apprehensions.

Leaders need to listen to understand what employees perceive is not working. As listening guru Carrol Suzuki of The Business of Listening explains, true listening is made up of a process of hearing, listening, and understanding in which the ears, head, and heart connect. There is no room for defensiveness here.

When employees feel their leader cares about their ideas and their concerns count, they become more open and are better able to see and acknowledge the things that are and are not working well, no matter how small they may appear at first. The leader's role is to listen and inquire about what needs to be shelved or done differently to move forward. In this atmosphere, people are more than willing to give their best.

Members of the team, meanwhile, can be more open to one another, discussing ways to solve the things that aren't working so well.

Part 3 of Our Story

A deep dive was initiated in which Brenda met with each member of the team independently and confidentially. She asked each the same solution-focused questions about the strengths of the team and individuals who stood out as emerging leaders, taking the time to listen to what they felt was needed for their team to heal and thrive. She also listened to complaints, treating them as windows to passionate views, personal values, and best hopes.

Following these interviews, Brenda synthesized the themes that emerged and shared them with the group in depth at a team retreat. The team decided by consensus which themes needed attention first. Solutions were generated by staff and supported by leadership. For the first time in a long time, staff were driving improvements that they were motivated to contribute to.

We recommend, almost simultaneously to any team intervention, having the team experiment with and ritualize ways that give voice to what is already working. Encouraging team members to do this and celebrating successes can bolster them to sustain the gains they make. As we have found time and time again, recognizing people for what they already are doing well helps them adapt to a new environment, respond more favourably to change, and grow. As we discussed in chapter two, "Find Greatness Everywhere: The Ten Dimensions of Greatness," *recognizing greatness is a non-negotiable element for healthy individuals and teams.*

Much like a natural ecosystem, a team environment can slowly become unhealthy, showing slight signs of trouble that may not initially be noticeable to the team itself because they work in it every day.

The team we have been profiling thought little could be done to help them. They had come to accept the status quo, in which inattention, lack of recognition, avoidance of accountability, and disrespectful behaviour were seen as "the ways things are around here."

Furthermore, they brushed all this off because they were so busy and attributed their frustration to external influences, imposed changes, seasonal shifts, short staffing, and the like. The team could have addressed issues more easily, if they had normalized as being part of a team the process of dealing with issues when they first arose, dealing with process, interpersonal, and structural disconnects while they were still small, isolated problems.

They say if you put a frog in a pot of boiling water, it will leap out right away to escape the danger. But if you put it in a kettle of cool water and *gradually* heat the kettle, the frog will not become aware of the threat until it is too late. The frog's survival instincts are geared toward detecting sudden changes, not subtle ones.

This is also true in humans. *People and teams often find themselves in trouble well after the problem has been simmering for a while.* The challenge is to pay attention not just to obvious threats but also to slowly developing ones.

It takes much greater intention, and sometimes greater courage, to deal with threats when they're not fires to fight but sparks with the *potential* to ignite. Team members sometimes need to take such a leap to demonstrate they can and will live into their best hopes and expectations, just as they hope their colleagues will take the leap with them.

Committing to Team Performance

Here are key strategies to honour the uniqueness of individuals on a team while also stimulating their energy and commitment to team performance. Any one of these can be foundational to build on.

1. Give Everyone a Voice

People at work may not expect to be loved by or be friends with all of their colleagues, but they do want to be understood and respected – respected for their voice and for what they think, believe, and feel. When they are heard, they feel part of something bigger than themselves. That sense of belonging yields opportunities for team members to contribute ideas and suggestions, and to build on one another's perspectives in a way that creates something bigger and stronger than what they could have contributed as individuals.

In this process, everyone's voice is viewed as important, regardless of role, experience, age, and so forth. We may need to draw out those who have been blamed, disrespected, undermined, or uninspired in the past. This may require taking the time to listen to complaints. When people feel their concerns are respected, they are more likely to use their voice, and are more likely to spark new insights.

2. Honour Greatness in the Moment

It is of key importance to practice the belief that every person has greatness, even in moments when they're not at their best. We can build on this by committing to acknowledge greatness when it is observed. Why think later that someone isn't complaining but simply pointing out that a project is losing momentum? Nothing ventured, nothing gained. Why not recognize this in the moment before the opportunity is lost? The person will be more likely to offer talents productively in new situations as a result.

Complain, Complain, Complain*

Sometimes we think of complainers as problems that have to be tolerated. What if we were to think instead of complaints as poorly worded requests? To think of complainers as very resourceful voices disguised as hostile ones takes some courage. What might we learn from people that could be helpful if we chose to listen differently to what was needed and wanted?

The next time someone complains to you, try listening intently without interruption and with support. Listen for three genuine compliments you could give. When you do this, it will probably take only two minutes or so before the person deescalates. Acknowledge authentically what the person has said by providing the compliments. (e.g., "Wow, Ted, you have clearly done a lot of problem-solving on this issue.")

When you hear and validate people, you create room for solutions to flourish. Explore together what the next step might be. It might be that they just needed to feel heard, or perhaps they will suggest an action that could be taken. Either way, they will be less likely to take such a hard stance next time.

As listeners, our energy is not dragged down by such negativity. Quite the opposite: it is replenished because we can see colleagues in a more resourceful light than if we had paid attention only to surface words and complaints.

* Based on an exercise in Nelson, Education and Training in Solution-Focused Brief Therapy.

---

3. Embrace Compliments

Compliments, as we described in chapter one, are a solution-focused way to attend to what is already working rather than what is not. In the box above we illustrated how to use compliments in order to make productive use of complaints. Similarly, receiving a compliment enables people to feel comfortable giving them.

It usually takes three seconds to turn a compliment into a weakness or neutralize it: *"Well, any professional would be good at problem-solving; it's part of the job."* Building a healthy team includes helping people to receive compliments well: *"Ted, I hear what you're saying, and it happens to be a strength you have in abundance. We need to benefit even more from your critical thinking."*

Eventually team members will respond to compliments not as uncomfortable or artificial statements but as a genuine and accepted part of how they interact with one another.

4. Find the Greatness in Every Person, No Exceptions

A true test of the FROG approach is acknowledging someone we do not see eye to eye with. We're not going to gel with everyone. However, more often than not, when we can look past what we don't like or agree with, put past differences aside, and suspend our pride for a moment, we can find it within ourselves to notice others' unique talents, passions, and virtues. And perhaps even offer a genuine compliment.

The individual we compliment may take notice and respond neutrally or positively. Over time, particularly when differences flare up, our attitude about the other person will begin to shift. We will more easily see the value they bring and understand that the differences are only one small piece of who they are. In fact, we may notice times when those differences are of benefit to the group.

When we refuse to believe some people are not worth our time, energy, or attention, we open ourselves up to seeing the greatness that resides in everyone.

5. Support Each Person to Expand their Greatness Reach

A solution-focused approach presupposes that everyone wants to do their best work every day. When that appears not to be happening, we can take it as a cue to figure out what is standing in the way. For example, we may see a creative person wilting and realize the disconnect: we have put her in a prescriptive job. What can we get her involved with so she can express her creativity? Or we see a relationship-oriented person in an isolated role. Perhaps we can empower her to help smooth things over between colleagues or arrange social events for the department.

Healthy team ecosystems are nurtured by the satisfied people who work in them, and satisfaction is the result of giving individuals' unique talents, passions, and virtues room to present themselves and grow.

A leader approached Sarah after a big project looking for the most meaningful way to recognize her team for defying the impossible, making it through a major project in record time. After exploring many options, she landed on writing personalized thank-you cards to each team member – over seventy of them!

It was a big time commitment. The leader was on board, with only one concern. "What if I can't find something positive to say about someone? We had a few pretty disruptive people."

Sarah offered the perspective that a complaint is merely a poorly worded request, so how could she recognize the greatness *behind* the complaint? This shifted something fundamental in this leader, who was struggling to rectify her normally strengths-based approach with her frustrated reactions when people were consistently negative.

She hypothesized that after these individuals felt their greatness was seen and validated, they might just turn their complaint-based approach into a more solution-oriented one. Guess what? She was right!

Got Thanks?

We've all had colleagues we didn't click with or had downright negative relationships with. We may have been able to work side-by-side with them, but it took incredible effort and energy to do so. Think of a person you are currently struggling with. List at least five strengths they have. Then reflect on these questions:

- Which strengths are similar to yours?
- Which are different?
- How might these similarities or differences be impacting how you think about and behave with this person?
- Which strength do you most admire and appreciate?
- In what ways does the person know this is admired and appreciated?
- What ways could this be expressed and demonstrated more explicitly?
- What might the benefit be to the relationship?
- What might the benefit be to the team?

Intrapersonal Greatness Creates Commitment

Most of us have experienced that, when people believe in us and acknowledge the great things we have to offer, we are more apt to contribute these things to the team's overall success. Intrapersonal greatness – confidence in our own individual greatness – is the gateway to stronger interpersonal relationships. When we think about commitment in the workplace, we think about things like:

- A demonstrated pledge to give something important of ourselves
- A promise or loyalty
- A good attitude
- A choice to stay with the team or organization when we're in demand elsewhere
- Speaking positively about the team or organization to others

Commitment is not just "showing up" at work; it is bringing all of our talents, passions, and virtues to contribute our best and feel the most fulfilled by the work. This is why loyalty is so important to cherish. If we don't value the greatness of others, they will save their best for other parts of their lives where it will be valued.

Part 4 of Our Story

Brenda realized the team needed some glue. She led the team through a "Commitment to My Colleagues" exercise, in which the team translated the themes from the deep dive to a list of important and specific commitments they needed to make in order to evolve. One staff member actually wrote a poem highlighting all the commitments and strengths discussed. (See next page.) The poem was posted on the wall in their area close to their daily communication huddle board.

Team members truly bought in to the commitments as they felt they owned them. Conversations and language changed. People felt more open to express their needs, compliment one another, and give appropriate feedback in respectful and timely ways.

Recognition and Retention

We've all heard the saying, *"People don't leave organizations; they leave managers."* We certainly hope people would leave if their organization

Let's take a moment

Reflect to the future

A few reminders on how we used to be

And can be again.

Help each other, communicate, teach, and learn.

Continue to work (the way we were raised).

Stand fast and faithful in what we do.

Listen to each other.

Look ahead to the future, don't dwell on the past.

Have compassion for each other.

Be honest and open. Share our concerns, but also try to forgive each other.

Remember, we are all different. We can accept this.

We all have had great days, many laughs, and many touching moments, so let's try to remember, and stay hopeful that they will come again.

Let's also remember those who have left us and appreciate the time we have had with them.

Some of have many years to go, others, not so much, but if we can stand together,

We can do anything.

doesn't address those rare abusive leaders out there. Most leaders, however, are a reflection of how they're treated and what the organization values and rewards.

If a steady stream of people is leaving a team or organization, a detailed review should be conducted to understand why. Exit interviews, reviews of satisfaction-survey results, and consulting remaining team members are good ways to start. Understanding what is working well is as important as understanding what is not; continuing to exercise elements of team legacy and rituals often help, providing much-needed glue during tough times. Furthermore, when we learn what the root issues are, how seriously do we commit to addressing them, one step at a time? How can studying teams that do not have these same root issues provide valuable insights to teams in trouble? For those who are all about the bottom line, consider this: How much does it cost organizations and teams when they lose good people? How hard is it to recruit replacements, and what downstream impact does this have on the business?

In our experience of working with hundreds of teams, a lack of meaningful recognition is not always the *root* issue but often is part of a culmination of factors that leave people feeling undervalued and uninspired. As we will see in the data presented in chapter five, "Think FROG on a Big Scale: How to Optimize Organizational Recognition," an analysis of an engagement dataset at our disposal tells us that 25% of those dissatisfied with recognition intend to leave their organizations. Studies tell us this figure increases when you lump in all the other factors indicative of a culture that doesn't value its people, period. Consider, for yourself, what would happen to your team's dynamics, productivity, and overall health if 25% or more of the members left tomorrow, next week, or even next month? Scary thought, right?

One person's decision to leave an unhealthy situation impacts a lot of people. It's to the team's benefit to find ways to recognize team members as a way to fuel a healthy culture. The healthiest teams we know are the ones most connected to their colleagues, knowing and acknowledging one another's unique talents, passions, and virtues. *When organizational recognition is done well, it reinforces and fuels the sense of connection, engagement, and loyalty.*

The Languages of Recognition

In the conclusion of this book, we invite you to take the Thirty-Day Recognition Challenge – noticing and acknowledging greatness at least once every day for a month – as a "recognition intention." Greatness is self-reinforcing. If you take on this challenge, you will find it easier to notice greatness very quickly in yourself and others. In Appendix A we give you lots of ways to recognize people, in case you're stuck for ideas; for that matter, whole books have been devoted to the subject, for example, *1001 Ways to Reward Employees* by Bob Nelson. We're guessing between our list and those in books like Bob's, you'll not run out of ideas.

To get you off on the right track, we want to reinforce that not everyone wants to be recognized in the same way. In their book *The 5 Languages of Appreciation in the Workplace*, Chapman and White share five broad approaches to recognition:

1. Words of affirmation: authentic verbal or written praise about accomplishments, character, or positive personality traits (given privately or publicly).

2. Quality time: undivided attention through quality conversations, shared experiences, small-group discussions, or working on a project together.

3. Acts of service: voluntary and genuine offers to help or doing something meaningful for someone when it is not asked or expected.

4. Tangible gifts: a gift the person cares about and that aligns with the importance of what is being recognized.

5. Physical touch: appropriate physical contact that matches what the receiver perceives as affirming.

The best place to start may be to figure out which of the five ways we like (see box, next page). This likely is how we'll show our appreciation of others, following the golden rule of treating others the way we wish to be treated. Better yet, why not follow the platinum rule, treating others the way *they* wish to be treated? Here are suggestions for how to figure this out:

- Talk one-on-one or as a team about recognition preferences; make it transparent (e.g., Mary says she likes hugs when she's having a hard day, so probably has a preference for physical touch)

- Observe others' behaviour; they probably recognize others in the way they like to be recognized (e.g., Tom gives written thank-you notes, so his preference is probably words of affirmation)

- Notice what team members request of others; what they ask for, suggest, and plan usually aligns with their preference (e.g., Laura is always planning social outings for the team outside of work, so her language is probably quality time)

- Listen to their complaints; if a complaint is simply a poorly worded request, what are they asking for that they're not getting? (e.g., Gary complains no one offers to help him when he is swamped and plans to stop offering to help others; he is probably craving acts of service)

How Are You Already Recognizing Others?

Looking at the list of the five languages of appreciation, reflect on how you see them in your workplace:

1. *Words of affirmation:*
2. *Quality time:*
3. *Acts of service:*
4. *Tangible gifts:*
5. *Physical touch:*

What could you do more of and who might respond well to this? What results would you expect?

Part 5 of Our Story

Among the most significant changes made on this team was hiring, as the new supervisor, the team member everyone believed was the strongest emerging leader. The team felt heard and validated, especially since teams in the organization had never been asked for input into these decisions.

The members of the team began to meet daily every morning, with staff leading the discussion, to set the plans for the day and solution-build issues from the day before. As a result of monitoring things they knew were important, the team saw a significant decline in their error rate, which they celebrated wholeheartedly. They made time for brief professional development lessons in which Brenda or a colleague taught five-minute segments on interpersonal skills to practice throughout the week. They debriefed what worked before layering on a new skill. They also reorganized every workstation, taking pride in the collaborative way they did it. The language of quality time really worked for the team.

To this day members of the team feel much more valued and see how their unique contributions fit the overall mission of their organization. Why? Because they feel confident they have made important improvements not just for themselves but for the safety of patients as a whole.

Teams as Ecosystems

We work more hours than play and spend more time at work than with our family, so we need to tend to our culture, our ecosystem, with the utmost care. Ecosystems can be delicate. People and organizations need to ensure they do not trample on one another's sacred space.

As with a frog egg, the cells of which must divide to survive and thrive, so too must individuals in the workplace be willing to embark on a metamorphosis. Some may be eager to adopt change, others may join in with the hope of what growth will bring, and still others may need more time because they feel vulnerable. Difficult times, when the survival of the team is the focus, may be frightening. However, seemingly minor signs of progress can fuel this delicate time of transition.

Just as a tadpole begins to grow a tail, subtle evidence of change can be discussed and celebrated in the work environment. This can take many forms. People may begin to use visuals, putting notes of recognition in public places, and make verbal acknowledgements (directly or perhaps when others are not present). Symbols of greatness may emerge. Traditions may be leveraged to solidify the types of things that will be recognized. Formal gatherings, such as staff meetings, may shift focus, such as making it a standing agenda item to ask for successes. Leadership meetings and retreats may incorporate a reflection of what people are proudest of since the last meeting and share learning and successes of their teams. Faith is built as recognition is ritualized as part of the journey.

Eventually, like the tadpole that continues to grow and becomes able to sustain itself outside of its original environment, with lungs and limbs forming into froglet form, a culture of recognition can become more self-sustaining. It is vulnerable at this point – don't get us wrong – but it is not as dependent on its original form.

Working creatively with others to incorporate what is valued, try new things, and discontinue what doesn't work builds strength and greater commitment to the future. People can begin to trust that, collectively, they will be able to use their talents to a greater extent. They can be more confident they are valued and wonder what else is possible. Carrying forward the parts of the past that work – seeing how much has been overcome already – helps alleviate anxiety.

Just as the froglet, in the middle of its metamorphosis, can live in water and on land, so too people may become increasingly curious about what is possible even while fearful of giving up the security of what is known.

The frog matures when nature dictates it can fully sustain itself. Human beings have a choice regarding how quickly they will adopt change, and if and when they will embrace it. In the ecosystem of the team, the stage of mature frog is reached when members are able to respect each individual and where they're at. Continued nurturing and exploration of new ways to acknowledge and recognize is essential to help all evolve, figuring out what each person uniquely needs.

Drastic changes in the ecosystem, or, worse, threatening it with toxins, can threaten the quality of life for all. While it's true human beings are highly adaptable, extreme exposure, especially over time, can threaten a team's co-existence – even a team that has a strong recognition culture. The team can sustain itself for a while, but if it does not tend to its survival, its culture is endangered. How the leader and colleagues seek clues and act on them nurtures the recognition journey and feeds its momentum.

As the recognition culture fully matures, all of the ingredients for sustaining and continuing growth are present. Team members adjust to change, and the ecosystem works more harmoniously.

Closing Reflection

What Does Recognition Look Like Right Now?
- *Where does recognition already happen in the team context? In what ways do members of the team ensure people feel valued and appreciated?*

- *In what specific ways is recognition ritualized? How is it built in to meetings, training, daily work, projects, and other systems?*

- *Who on the team is demonstrating great aptitude and authenticity in recognition? What is it about them that works so well? How might this be replicable? To what extent do they know the important impact they're having on the team? How could this be made even clearer?*

- *How are complaints and "complainers" treated on the team? To what extent might there be opportunities to leverage the greatness within the complaints?*

- Do people value compliments and practice them? What might happen if they happened more, differently, consistently?
- How ready is the team to embrace recognition? What is one small step any individual or the collective could take to foster this further as part of the culture?

Inspiration for **Action**

Recognition is the greatest motivator.

–GERRALD EAKEDARDE

People respond in accordance to how you relate to them.

–NELSON MANDELA

Recognition is not a scarce resource. You can't run out of it.

–SUSAN M. HEATHFIELD

Brains, like the heart, go where they are appreciated.

–ROBERT McNAMARA

Twenty years from now you will be more disappointed by the things you didn't do than by the ones you did. So throw off the bowlines. Sail away from the safe harbor. Catch the trade winds in your sails. Explore. Dream. Discover.

–MARK TWAIN

People work for money but go the extra mile for recognition, praise and reward.

–DALE CARNEGIE

Appreciation can make a day, even change a life. Your willingness to put it into words is all that is necessary.

–MARGARET COUSINS

People may take a job for more money, but they often leave it for more recognition.

–BOB NELSON

Five

Think FROG on a Big Scale: How to Optimize Organizational Recognition

Opening Reflection

The goal of this chapter is to help you understand the linkage across organizations between recognition and employee engagement, morale, and productivity. Looking at a slice of the workforce, for example by analyzing engagement survey databases from hundreds of organizations, what can be understood regarding low- vs. high-rated organizations? What could you do armed with these insights? How do you think recognition would help your organization to increase employee engagement and, consequently, well-being and productivity?

*On a scale of 10 to 1, with 10 standing for **"The organization I work for does everything it can to create and preserve a culture of recognition"** and 1 being the opposite of that, where do you think your organization is now?*

10	9	8	7	6	5	4	3	2	1

What does the organization already do that works? What are you already doing that contributes to this positive recognition culture? How do you reinforce and contribute to a healthy culture every day? Where would you like the organization to be? Where would you like your organization to be on the scale? Imagine it is one step higher. What is it doing differently?

It was a pivotal day when Kim Shepherd, now the CEO of Decision Toolbox, realized what effective organizational recognition looked like.

About twenty years ago, Kim was offered a promotion from middle management. She was surprised and thrilled. There was only one catch: her guaranteed bonus would be replaced by an executive compensation bonus system (i.e., if the company didn't do well, she would get no bonus at all). She thought it over and decided to take the plunge. When bonus time came around, she expected to get one as the company had been doing well. She couldn't have been more surprised, however, to see a *very* substantial amount show up in her bank account.

As Kim relates this story, it wasn't the amount of money that was most meaningful to her (although that didn't hurt); it was the impact of discovering the bonus in a way she didn't expect.

"They could have sent me a cheque in the mail, but then it would have been all about the money," Kim says. "It was the surprise of going to my bank account and seeing it sitting there, thinking it was a mistake at first, then my surprise turning into appreciation for the way the gesture was made. They wanted my first bonus to be meaningful. Before that I thought recognition was only about the human touch. That is really important, and money can be, too, as long as it creates 'exponential energy.'"

People like Kim realize meaningful recognition has a "big bang." It has the power to represent the essence of what needs to be recognized, which burns itself into the spirit and consciousness of the person being recognized. Put another way, in Kim's case, if you want to communicate to your newest member, *"You have wowed us this year,"* then wow her in how you recognize her.

"At Decision Toolbox, we know anyone can pull you in to a cubicle and give you a raise or say 'good job,'" Kim says. "That's a lost opportunity. You need to make the gesture so meaningful it infuses energy into that person so they can do even more of what is clearly already working. Never pass up an opportunity to recognize big."

You may be thinking it's okay for Kim to give time to recognition because she has a small business and ample time. Wrong. Decision Toolbox is a multi-million-dollar company on a growth trajectory with over a hundred staff located across the United States. Kim says creating and preserving a great culture is the single most important thing she does as CEO, and recognition is an essential part of a great culture.

"Meaningful recognition in a way that cultivates a healthy organizational culture doesn't happen off the corner of your desk. You need to stop, slow down, and think about the biggest way you can do it. The payoff from what you get back from your staff, not to mention the high you have as the person behind the recognition, is worth all the time and effort you devote to planning that recognition."

You may also be thinking it's okay for profitable private sector organizations to think this way but what about fiscally restrained or not-for-profit organizations? Kim's story, you may have noticed, was not about the dollar figure but about the importance the organization placed on recognizing big. Another example of a company that made a big gesture with little cost is one that sent a bouquet of roses to the wife of an employee in thanks for her understanding regarding how frequently the organization required her husband to travel that month. The flowers weren't for him, but the message was clear: appreciation of the sacrifices his family needed to make to support him so his full talents were available to the organization and its clients at a critical time.

The cool thing about these stories is that they are doable by any company, no matter their size, history, operating structure, financial situation, or industry. Every business can create exponential energy through meaningful recognition. Unfortunately, it doesn't happen often enough. We've covered in previous chapters how recognition can and should start with each of us; greatness is most deeply felt when it comes from within and among those we trust and respect. That doesn't leave organizations off the hook, however. Organizations have the opportunity to harness and grow the best from their talent through Kim's concept of exponential energy.

It is essential for organizations to commit to doing recognition well, in ways that fit the culture's purpose and the greatness of employees. This chapter contains ample evidence for why recognition cannot be ignored. We encourage you to ponder what you and your organization might experiment with. Note, though, that you'll never create a recognition culture if you get caught up looking for the perfect recipe. Open the cookbook and start trying the recipes already there.

Getting Clear: What Employees Want

When Canadian survey company Metrics@Work analyzed its database of a quarter of a million staff engagement surveys from hundreds of companies, the results on recognition were disheartening. (See also Appendix C.) Of all the organizations that chose to ask about recognition, it was the lowest of the twenty-five most commonly ranked drivers of engagement. No wonder organizations don't always ask about recognition, and rarely ask how employees want to be recognized.

This is so unfortunate. Organizations are missing an opportunity right in front of their noses to increase engagement. Of all the variables that are commonly studied in employee engagement surveys, the topic of rewards and recognition is the fourth most correlated with it, behind trust in the organization, satisfaction with senior leadership, and continuous quality improvement.* In fact, all of these variables correlate, so a more tangible focus on recognition would be an effective way to increase trust as well as satisfaction with senior leadership. Those who work in continuous improvement cultures know it is ideas and solutions from staff that form the basis of daily improvements. It follows that these gains must be celebrated.

If this doesn't seem like sufficient evidence for the business case (let alone the human case we have been presenting in previous chapters), consider this as well: employees are 25% more likely to remain in the organization when they're recognized. It stands to reason that they stay in their department with their direct supervisor when they feel what they have to offer is valued and needed. Many factors contribute to a person's decision to leave the organization. However, if an organization has a turnover issue, or the trend is heading that way, it would be worthwhile to consider, perhaps even by asking about it in exit interviews, how recognition in their work areas and in the organization as a whole might have helped.

How come this is not part of the broader discourse of business the way work-life balance is? Let's hope it's not because we still think recognition is just fluffy stuff. We hope you, our readers, will help change any such perception.

A common thread in the story of the top-rated companies in Canada, such as Aecon Group, Nuance Communications, TD Bank, and others, is not their size or fame but their strong focus on recognizing and leveraging the best in their people. Smaller players are also making a big splash on quality of work life, including SAS Institute, BCG Consulting, and Admiral Insurance. As with Kim's company, mammoth size is not

---

* Trust in the organization r=.766; Satisfaction with Senior Management r=.677; Continuous Quality Improvement .659; Employee Recognition = .644

necessary in order to make major inroads in cultivating healthy organizational culture. Another thing common to the top-rated companies is that they get the best from their talent, which also translates into healthy bottom lines.

Brenda's son-in-law works for a very small company in downtown Toronto. Early on, the employees, all of whom are in their twenties, made it a business practice that each employee would recognize someone else in the company at the end of every month. They looked forward to this time when they could check in with each other about how they were doing. As business picked up, the practice diminished. It was the team members themselves who noticed the difference and requested that this recognition practice be renewed and be given top priority.

Recognition is important in the not-for-profit sector, as well, where large mandates and limited funds require a constant focus on how to stretch dollars and use them most efficiently.

What do we do if we don't work for one of the big companies? After all, not everyone is able to work for those at the "top." Many of us have dedicated our careers to the public sector and helping professions, which seem not to make it onto these lists. Are we bound to the fate of accepting a less than ideal company culture? You can probably guess our answer is no. As we have been exploring in this book, each one of us reinforces and contributes to a healthy culture every day. *We can become cultural anthropologists within our organization. When we focus on the nuances of what works in our unique culture, we're more likely to contribute our efforts in an intentional way.*

It's in the Data: What Staff Say They Need and Want Most

In looking more deeply at the engagement survey dataset, we see a big difference in how well recognition is done at interpersonal, team, and organizational levels. The highest average recognition score of an organization was 80% satisfied and the lowest 29% satisfied. That is a huge range (a statistically significant one, for those of you who like statistics). Which type of organization would *you* like to work for?

What do we know about the differences between the high-scoring vs. low-scoring organizations? Before we tell you what we found, we'd like to ask what you think the differences are, based on your experience.

What Separates Low-Recognition from High-Recognition Organizations?

1. Based on your work experience, what you know of other organizations, and what your friends and family have to say about the organizations they work for, what do you think are the differences between companies with higher recognition scores and those with lower ones?

Low-Recognition Organizations   **High-Recognition Organizations**
- –   –
- –   –
- –   –
- –   –
- –   –

2. If you had to guess where your organization would fall, how satisfied would you guess employees would rate it? Mark your thoughts below.

0%	50%	100%

How satisfied people are in your organization

It probably won't surprise you that organizational characteristics associated with highest satisfaction are linked to recognition. Employees who were the most highly recognized report they are more:*
- Engaged in their job overall
- Engaged with the broader organization
- Involved with and in decision-making
- Satisfied with senior leaders
- Trustful of the organization
- Involved in improving how work was done (as was their whole team)
- Innovative (as was their whole team)
- Satisfied with communication
- Aware of performance feedback and feel performance is managed
- Satisfied with opportunities for advancement
- Likely to stay with the organization

Did you list similar characteristics? We bet you did. After all, you've probably experienced at least one of the two extremes, and when you have, it is hard to forget.   * All results were statistically significant.

Could the difference between high- and low-scoring organizations really impact engagement that much? Staff members say it does. We clustered the recognition-satisfaction results into the top third, middle third, and bottom third. Where staff report the highest satisfaction with rewards and recognition, organizational engagement scores on average are 80%. Where they report the lowest satisfaction, the scores on average are 47%. This brings up the question: How much more must staff be contributing in their jobs when they work in an environment with a strong emphasis on recognizing the value they contribute and their unique greatness?

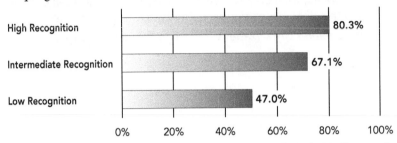

Engagement in Organizations with High, Medium, and Low Recognition Satisfaction Scores

It is clear that focusing on and practicing recognition helps organizations whose staff are walking out the door. An average of 78% were likely to stay in organizations where people rated the highest satisfaction with recognition; the figure was only 65% for those who were in the middle and 47% for those who felt they were not recognized. If we think about the cost of recruitment, time needed to hire, train, and mentor new staff, and loss of organizational knowledge, the difference can seem a whole lot bigger than the numerical difference of 31%.

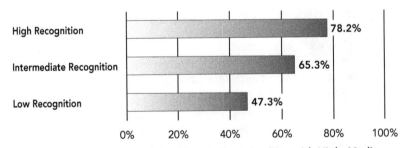

Intention to Stay in Organizations with High, Medium, and Low Recognition Satisfaction Scores

Remember our friend Kim Shepherd, CEO of a dynamic, growing recruitment firm? She says leaders need to prioritize recognition. "If you are a true leader who cares about this stuff, you have to devote the majority of your critical thinking to this." It appears this is not a consistently held belief or practice on the part of senior leaders, because the highest-scoring organizations have an average satisfaction of 72% and the lowest average below 30%. Remember, hundreds of organizations are in this dataset, so we're not talking about just a few leaders, but thousands. *We can learn a lot from leaders who are practicing the art of recognizing greatness, including how much it helps them leverage the talent they work with.*

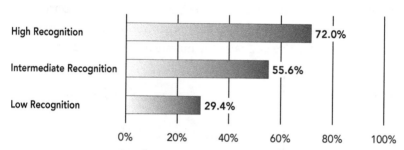

Satisfaction with Senior Leadership in Organizations with High, Medium, and Low Recognition Satisfaction Scores

You may think Kim is more successful with engagement and recognition than CEOs or managers with a more autocratic leadership style. But just because Kim is big on the human side of things doesn't mean she's wishy-washy. She makes a strong business case for investment in talent. *She sees it as her job as CEO to do whatever she can to build energy and creativity, not deplete it, so business goals can be met and surpassed.* We have mentioned the talent shortage several times in this book, but it is important to repeat again as it further drives the business case for recognition.

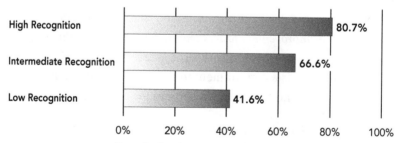

Trust in Organizations with High, Medium, and Low Recognition Satisfaction Scores

Let's look at one more interesting driver of engagement: continuous improvement. We have worked for organizations that have a continuous improvement LEAN focus and those that do not. We can tell you first-hand that cultures that practice continuous improvement will have humble leaders, empowered and involved staff, shared decision-making structures, and standardized but nimble processes. Teams celebrate both small successes and the identification of problems as opportunities to improve. Those doing the work are considered the most valuable asset. They are the ones who can identify the hundreds of small opportunities to make improvements that make their organizations more competitive and more cost-effective and raise the morale of staff and customers.

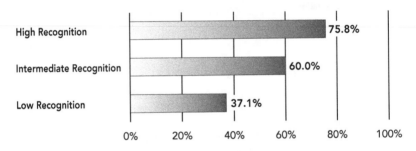

Continuous Improvement in Organizations with High, Medium, and Low Recognition Satisfaction Scores

Not surprisingly, recognition goes hand in hand with a continuous improvement culture. Those who say they work in this type of culture respond with a 75% satisfaction rate with recognition vs. those who work in other less participatory cultures, where the rate comes in at less than 40% satisfied with recognition. The other element to consider is how sophisticated the organization is in adopting a solution-focused continuous improvement culture. *The partnership of a focus on solutions and continuous improvement fosters and sustains results, motivating and engaging staff to create the positive effect that every organization desires.* Such a partnership is a commitment to continuous improvement with a focus on success and the strengths and unique contributions of all.

Learning from Successes

Let's also examine the companies that score well in *how* they are succeeding. What are they doing that works? We have insights to share because the regular pulse checks we do in our work tell us what employees have to say.

The people at one municipality we spoke with say they're glad they conducted a pulse check (through an engagement survey), because a rude awakening led to corrective action that created great results.

The City of Markham serves an urban population of 300,000 people, employing hundreds to provide a wide range of services from community centres to garbage pickup to marriage licences. Over the years, the City conducted engagement surveys and tried a few things to improve morale, but didn't make significant inroads. In 2012, that all changed.

A new Chief Administrative Officer was not okay with the fact that the latest survey results showed engagement scores had dropped yet again; the executive team specifically targeted recognition as a strategic priority, charging a new cross-sectional Employee Appreciation Team with the important task of implementing recognition that *staff* said they valued and wanted.

What did the municipal managers do? Based on their own ideas and those they received from staff:

1. They set out to find out what wasn't working with previous strategies and what could be salvaged. They brushed off a Recognition Toolbox (containing birthday cards, movie passes, and other things to recognize staff on the fly). Instead, they taught leaders *how* to use such things to recognize people one-on-one. They helped leaders understand it wasn't giving the card or gift that was most important but the personalized thank you that went with it.

2. They invited all staff to get involved in branding the new recognition program in a fun, organization-wide naming campaign. The RISE (Recognizing Incredible Staff Endeavours) program was the winning submission by a staff member who became the face of the program with her picture on posters and the website. She also received a prize, as did a number of others for honourable mentions.

3. They had each department identify at least one improvement project. Departmental Directors were held accountable for progress and to give monthly updates to the executive team on evidence of meaningful progress.

4. They encouraged leaders to hold regular team meetings and ensured that recognition of one another, and not just by the leader, was a regular agenda item.

5. They launched an annual Teamwork Day, breaking down silos by having cross-sectional staff attend a morning or afternoon session with a

high-quality motivational speaker; teams that had made significant strides in increasing their satisfaction presented or created professional quality videos to share what they worked on to increase engagement, allowing others to learn from and celebrate with them.

6. They nominated teams for awards for the work they were doing to improve their team culture and received the award in celebration style on Teamwork Day.

It doesn't seem like rocket science; however, there are some subtle differences in how leaders shook up recognition at the corporate level:

1. They ensured that the senior team felt passionate about recognition and communicated this focus clearly to all.

2. They didn't allow excuses, such as, *"My department is too big,"* when goals weren't met or did not align with the organization's strategic direction. They had influential leaders role model their commitment to improving recognition within their portfolio and report back on the measurable impact it was making.

3. They didn't wait for the perfect time, knowing there would never be one.

4. They measured results and trends over time, making those results transparent, including what was being done about them, so people could see progress.

5. They kept looking for ways to do things better. For example, internal communication was an issue so they searched for new technologies, explored what other organizations were doing, and solicited employee ideas until they found strategies that began to improve satisfaction.

6. They branded recognition to help employees see all the things associated with it. For example, the City had a wellness program but staff didn't associate it with recognition.

7. They found out the types of recognition that mattered most to employees, ensured leaders knew them, too, and provided leaders with the skills and tools to deliver.

In summary, what contributed to success in this case and others can be highlighted as:

- Keeping the things that worked and acknowledging pockets where there were positive things to learn
- Changing what wasn't working based on what staff saw as most important

- Creating new ways to recognize staff and teams, driven by the work of a team of staff, with the leaders' role being to support and follow through

Sounds like the basic assumptions of a solution-focused approach, doesn't it?

1. If it isn't broken, don't fix it.

2. If something is working, do more of it.

3. If something isn't working, try something different.

As we discussed in chapter four, "Enable Greatness with Healthy Team Ecosystems," there are essential strategies for the teams in an organization particularly low in engagement that need to be implemented at a local level. Once again, teams that excel in meeting certain guidelines can be showcased and asked to share their successes with others. Otherwise, corporate recognition may fail to make significant inroads. It's not an either/or but a both/and for those significantly in need.

Connecting the Dots

The case story of the City of Markham above is a great example of the formula Gostick and Elton share in their book *The Orange Revolution*, from their Carrot series on recognition. They have found the most effective leaders follow the formula of what they call Basic 4 + Recognition:

> **Goal setting**
> **Communication**
> **Trust**
> **Accountability**
> **+ Recognition.**

They stress that recognition needs the strong foundation of the first four elements in the formula for it to be effective and meaningful. Team members give their best when the person they report to:

- Clearly outlines what needs to be achieved
- Listens well and speaks up
- Acts in a trustworthy manner
- Believes in others
- Follows through on what she says will be done

It makes sense. If one minute we feel buoyed by recognition that exactly fits what we need, and then are let down, we may become confused or distrustful of the very person who has recognized us, whether a leader or a colleague. The result? The power of that recognition falls flat.

Furthermore, goal setting, communication, trust, accountability, and recognition happen more naturally when there are fewer barriers. This is why we say it's important to start from a place of greatness. Environments where people can do their best work find ways for each member to continue to evolve their contribution so it best matches their talents, passions, and virtues. There is a strong belief in these environments that people can and will do their best when given the chance.

Getting Real About Your Organization's Approach to Recognition

Reflect on your own organization using the questions below. How many resonate? Perhaps they are the reason you picked this book up in the first place.

- *Do your recognition programs feel fresh?*
- *Do people still use the recognition programs as they were intended (e.g., names are forwarded for awards requiring nominations)?*
- *Do people pay attention to who receives recognition?*
- *Do people know the various ways the organization recognizes people and teams?*
- *Does corporate recognition feel meaningful at an individual level?*
- *Do people believe there is a fair process for determining who gets recognized?*
- *In engagement surveys, do results show recognition efforts are working?*
- *In engagement surveys, do people say they feel recognized for the work they do?*
- *Are there clear methods for recognition across the organization?*

"No" answers to any of the questions above may indicate it is time to take another look at organizational recognition.

We're not suggesting it's easy to start from a place of greatness. It often requires a shift in the mindset of individuals and the approach of the organization. As Marcus Buckingham argues in his series of books on strengths, we miss the mark when we begin by looking for and inevitably finding evidence of deficits. The alternative is to start from a place of where strengths already exist and talents, passions, and virtues have already revealed themselves and are present, so it's just a matter of acknowledging and reinforcing them in everyday work.

Recognition Strategies for Hitting the Mark

1. Stay in Touch

Depending on the size of the organization, recognition events often are coordinated by a department or a few people. People specifically responsible for recognition need to know the important role they play in building and sustaining a strong culture. As we have already discussed, no one can be delegated this responsibility alone. The healthiest organizations have people across the organization do this daily.

But what if the people in charge of this just stay in their office? What happens if they are seen as simply reinforcing their own policies and agenda and/or are visible only at the recognition event itself? What impression does all this leave? It should never be a surprise when people are satisfied or dissatisfied with recognition. *Recognition is not a program to administer, a task to check off the to-do list, or a working group duty. It's a culture that shifts with small changes that can only happen with people.*

It may not be happening enough, but it *is* happening. There are pockets in organizations of every type and size where people prioritize the personalized acknowledgement of greatness. Where is it already happening in your organization? What practices are leading to measurable successes such as high employee engagement, employee retention, and customer satisfaction?

Although it would be a pleasure to be recognized by people at all levels within an organization, employees, in general, most want their direct supervisor to recognize them. In contrast, corporate recognition events reinforce the *organization's* focus on recognition. A question for leaders, therefore, is: When was the last time you spent at least half a day out of your office with people who do the value-adding work (e.g., deliver service to the customer, make the product, etc.)? If you can't remember such a time, you probably can anticipate what we're about to say. Every leader needs to spend time *with staff in* their environment. There are several important reasons for this. When leaders are present, they:

- Show staff they care about the work they do and want to help them deliver the value they are capable of
- Get to know what energizes their staff and teams, and what deflates them
- Begin to gain the trust of staff and teams so there is an honest dialogue
- Know what factors staff feel are worth recognizing and how they like to be recognized
- Have the pulse of the organization (and won't be surprised when the next survey results come out)

So You Want to Know What I Think?

Suppose you take our advice and decide you're going to find out what staff members really think about corporate recognition. Use a FROG lens (not that it's the only way to transform your corporate recognition program) and ask the following questions. Brace yourself for the truth and get pumped to do something with the richness of information you will receive.

- When was the last time you were FROGed? What was it for? What do you think was the most important value you contributed to the organization?
- Where are the missed opportunities for you to be recognized?
- When was the last time you FROGed someone?
- If you could change how recognition happens in the organization, what would you do?
- What is one important way for recognition to spread across the organization such that it motivates people to do their best?
- What positive impact have you or the people you work with experienced from existing organizational recognition programs?
- Has the organization put in place recognition programs that actually had the opposite effect?

Visible leadership is a foundational element of strong recognition cultures. We're at a loss to think of a single leading team or organization where leaders have little connection to staff and recognition comes only from the ranks.

There is no perfect formula for how much time is enough or ideal to spend with staff. To be honest, most leaders with a big portfolio feel they never have as much time as they would like or need. However, some is better than none. And rather than head for the hills when staff open up to you with their honest opinion, accept that this is their way of saying, "*I trust you.*" The earliest signs of this may feel counterintuitive, for example, when they:

- Tell you what's really going on – perhaps things you don't want to hear
- Disagree with you
- Don't scatter when you come around
- Make suggestions without being asked
- Introduce you to others by name (rather than as "the boss")
- Smile when they see you

The same goes for support departments that assist others who deliver value to the customer directly or produce the programs or products other departments deliver, as it does for leaders. Are support departments aware they can add value to the departments they support and their internal customers? Do they deliver? Is there something they could do more of or differently to succeed in delivering greater value?

When we as leaders stay in touch so we can recognize effectively at an individual, team, and organizational level, we ensure that we are connected to those doing value-added work. This demonstrates to everyone that recognition doesn't exist because *"all organizations have to do something."* Rather, it becomes a genuine and authentic marker of the importance of internal talent in the overall functioning of the organization. (The leaders know it, and they want everyone else to know it, too.)

2. Focus Daily on What's Working

Continuous improvement cultures traditionally focus on identifying problems and working to solve them. Sometimes this is misconstrued. People believe only negatives are being sought. When the focus is disproportionately on what is not working, the feeling may be that the broken processes are the fault of staff.

However, using a solution-focused approach, the problems can be identified *and* what is studied is when or where the problems *do not* exist. People are encouraged to build solutions from this vantage point. They are empowered to generate ideas and move forward with them. When improvements result, these successes are replicated so they become the best standards to follow.

Fortunately, there are countless examples of cultures in which continuous improvement is conducted in an empowering way, cultures in which employees know their input is important and necessary. This helps explain why there is such a high correlation in continuous improvement cultures between engagement and recognition.

For one example, consider shifting the way Lydia and Jessica from chapter three handled their work processes. What if, instead of focusing on that rare time when their results were late, they worked in an environment where such an incident caused people to study the last time samples *weren't* late or even were early? Wouldn't this soften the guilt Lydia and Jessica may be feeling and motivate them? Equally important, wouldn't they learn about what to reinforce in their processes to keep the system working well? Building on what is *already* working becomes a call to action to address the times when it isn't, in a way that engages the front line and builds solutions from within.

Employees and leaders alike need to be able to feel that, when they do bring up legitimate issues (however they define that), they are heard and valued and the issue is followed through on. The most important thing is to empower them to make changes as they see fit (after all, they do the work every day). Putting it in their hands to make the change happen and giving the necessary resources (e.g., a small budget) and time away from their work is a great way to say they are valued.

Here are some of the best ways to ensure employee commitment to making improvements:

- Believe staff when they bring up an issue; take it seriously
- Follow through on what you say you're going to do (or explain why you can't)
- See "complainers" as people with poorly worded requests
- Focus more time and energy on those who are performing than those who are not
- Provide staff with the resources to be successful

- Acknowledge efforts, even "unsuccessful" ones, that can be the basis of learning
- Look for what's working
- Celebrate small successes

Supporting staff to make improvements, even if they aren't exactly what the leader would do, says, *"I know you have talents and ideas of how to address this issue, and I believe you will make a positive difference."* The more leaders are present in the work environment, the more people will see their support as authentic. As a bonus, trust will flourish.

3. Pay Attention

There are all kinds of signs that employees feel underappreciated and unrecognized. An easy clue is an increase in turnover. If they aren't doing so already, organizations should monitor turnover rates regularly as an indicator of how healthy the climate is. By looking for trends (i.e., three data points in a row), they will know whether they need to put a plan in place to turn a growing problem around.

High turnover rates don't just mean a team is in trouble but offer a sign of a bigger problem that needs to be addressed before it is so extensive it does long-term damage to the people and the business. However, and it is a big however, it is also important to look at the teams where turnover is low. What is keeping these staff engaged, committed, and loyal to their team and the organization? How could we take what we learn from these teams to assist those that are struggling?

Be somewhat cautious about exit interviews, however. While they are a helpful tool to learn why people are leaving, employees have little vested interest in telling the truth when they're on their way out the door. They may be worried they will get a bad reference, not feel their feedback will make a difference, or simply not be invested enough to bother. Decentralized exit interviews, in which the employee is interviewed by an employee they trust, with the results being pooled by HR, are the best way we've found to find out the real reason why people are leaving. Oh, and you know you're really in trouble if turnover is so bad that you're too busy recruiting to investigate it!

But imagine if we also studied why people stay. Interviewing people who stay can provide a wealth of information. The questions could be:

- What keeps you here?
- What keeps you loyal after all these years?
- What energizes you most?

The answers may lead to the secrets of success and be clues to apply in other areas.

As we referenced earlier, another obvious sign employees feel under-appreciated shows up not just in low engagement survey scores but also, just as importantly, in a low percentage of surveys actually completed. Engaged employees often take the time to fill out surveys; disengaged, distrustful, or skeptical employees (e.g., *"Nothing will be done with the information anyway"*) may not bother. Furthermore, how can an orga-nization feel confident in a survey's results if just a few people answered the survey? Were they the happy people or just the dissatisfied ones? Did they feel pressured to do so or genuinely want to? Low response rates result in data that are unreliable (and waste fiscal resources).

Again, find out what works. Where in the organization are the largest numbers of surveys filled out? How did staff manage to take the time? What allowed them to be so trusting? We can learn a lot from successes.

In the case of a high enough response rate but results that tell a grim tale of dissatisfaction, hope need not be lost. At least the concerns are clear, or clearer than they were before the survey was completed. More in-depth study may be necessary to understand this qualitatively.

Here are some tips for increasing response rates:

- Focus on the *why*; ensure the intention and purpose are solid, then share them
- Explain what will be done with results; be transparent
- Promise a date and method for employees getting a summary of the feedback
- Have a contest between departments for 100% compliance rate
- Explain what was done since the last survey
- Have "influencers" in departments help plan how the survey is rolled out and what will be done with results; this way they can talk genuinely about the survey being an opportunity and communicate the value they see in tallying survey results
- Ensure the survey asks about strengths, resources, and successes

To increase response rates for future surveys:

- Disseminate results quickly and fully
- Follow through; ensure employees see something is being done as a result of the survey
- Celebrate and showcase what is working in teams
- Celebrate progress teams have made over time

When survey results are in, make sure you do something with them. We've discussed team strategies and described the City of Markham as an example of an organizational approach. As a leader, you can support the spirit of increasing recognition in how you engage with staff after results come out. When in the work environment, speak with people about what the results confirmed for them, what surprised them, what they think should be the initial focus for improvement, and how they think high results can be maintained. Even when people come across as negative, you have the opportunity to genuinely thank them for taking the time to provide their feedback and then ask them for solutions. *Apathy is the enemy of engagement, and recognition is the shield.*

Customers See Everything, Including When It's Working...

Even in high-turnover industries such as esthetics, there are "positive anomalies" from which much can be learned.

Brenda recently returned to a hair salon where she had not been a customer for fifteen years. She was immediately greeted by most who worked there and was amazed the same people had stayed in their jobs for so long. Despite the salon having changed locations three times, the staff followed the owner. When Brenda asked them what kept them so loyal, they said:

- *The owner recognizes us as individuals and treats us with respect*
- *He expects us to work hard but is consistently fair*
- *He is very understanding when we need time off*
- *The work environment is fun*
- *We are like a family*
- *We laugh and cry together*
- *We support one another through the good times and bad*

---

4. Make It All About Talent in the Organization

In many organizations, we have seen corporate recognition programs built around the organization's values and strategic directions. Seems like a good idea in theory: The organizations are recognizing what they want to see more of. They believe their values are always positive, so what's the problem? The reality is, for most, such programs just don't resonate. Some in the organization may not even know what the values and strategic directions are, and those who do may or may not believe the organization actually lives by them. Even if they do, there often is low ownership of these awards as they are grounded in what the *organization* feels is important.

Whether it is at a team level or organizational level, working *with* staff to identify what should be recognized is a significant step in building meaning into the awards. Don't be afraid to change them up, too, especially when someone comes up with a great idea. As we discussed in chapter four, "Enable Greatness Through Healthy Team Ecosystems," small, quirky gestures can have a big impact. Something as simple as handing out little squishy frogs and telling someone, *"FROG stands for Forever Recognize Others' Greatness, and the greatness I see in you is..."* can begin a subtle movement of recognizing greatness in the moment. Similarly, if someone says, *"We should give each other a pat on the back,"* support that staff member to try out a "Pat on the Back" award and see what happens.

If broad-based recognition is not wrapped up in extensive planning, ceremony, and expenses, it's easy to keep it "fresh." Notice we said broad-based, not formal. Corporate recognition doesn't have to be stuffy to be considered organizational recognition.

Don't forget to ask staff *how* people want to be recognized. People may want free parking, gift certificates, a day off with pay, lunch with the CEO, or a whole host of other options. Don't be afraid to share what your budget is and ask employees how they would spend it. Maybe even present a few options, ask for a few others, and then publish the results. Make a big deal over how it is a shared opportunity to plan an important element of organizational culture together.

Practice humility as an organization. *Be students of your own organizational culture. Keep the things that work (for many) and try some new things.* Show people their ideas matter by showcasing them for a period of time and gauging feedback. You don't have to find the perfect solution right off the hop, if it even exists. If something seems to get great results, keep it going. If not, try something else. Remember, people can detect a dog and pony show and may not want to participate, let alone value what is being awarded.

When we look at the results of how people most want to be recognized, it's very clear. Topping the list are verbal thank yous (89%), private words of praise (84%), and written thank yous (82%). Although these are easiest on a one-on-one level, how much "exponential energy" could be built were these things to happen on a larger scale?

I Must Thank...Are you Kidding Me?

Sarah recently facilitated a leadership retreat with some colleagues that focused on building resiliency in a team that had undergone a great deal of change. One of the many strategies taught was the power of personalized recognition. All leaders received five blank thank-you cards and were asked to write a genuine acknowledgement to five or more leader colleagues (they could ask for more cards if they wanted to write more).

Oh, the outcry! Some said it was like high school – would some not get a Valentine? Some felt it was childish. Others felt they were too busy. Needless to say, assurances were required (*"Trust us on this one...it will work"*).

The executive team wrote one for every leader and as it turned out every leader did receive at least one card from a colleague without there being a structure to ensure this. In the end, participants said the most memorable and helpful part of the whole retreat was the part they had resisted the most: receiving genuine, specific acknowledgements written by colleagues. Leaders to this day tell Sarah they pull these cards out when they need a lift or visual reminders of how valued they are by those they work with.

5. Watch for Unintended Consequences

We worked for an organization that decided it was going to do away with their old ways of recognizing: giving people length-of-service pins, having a sit-down dinner, and giving jewellery gift certificates. We were told people didn't like the pins, often had a time conflict with the dinner so couldn't go, and, in many cases, weren't using their gift certificates.

The company ended up reducing the ceremony portion, changing the meal to a bigger buffet selection, making the dress casual, and offering a catalogue of gifts.

We ran into unintended consequences. The choice of gifts and outfits did not equal meaningful engagement to employees. They felt the changes were only about cuts. Mostly, they were resentful no one asked them first. All valid points. Another lesson: just because people are unhappy with the status quo doesn't mean they'll like the new way any better, especially when they haven't been part of shaping the new way.

Instead of seeing us as listening and being responsible with funds, people felt disrespected and devalued. We had listened to what wasn't working for a few and forgot to focus on what *was* working for most. We also needed to ask them what, if anything, they would prefer instead. We assumed the changes would have a positive impact, particularly when we worked hard to plan a corporate recognition program grounded in what we had taken the time to learn employees valued most.

According to the work of Robert Merton, unintended consequences can take one of three forms:

1. A positive benefit that is not expected (e.g., reduced "silos" between departments when all group recognition activities were brought together organization-wide).

2. A negative, detrimental impact in addition to the desired impact (e.g., anger about "losing" unique recognition events as a team while also appreciating being able to celebrate with people from other departments they're not used to seeing socially).

3. A negative, detrimental impact contrary to the original desired impact (e.g., anger toward administration for taking team-recognition events away and amalgamating them into one).

Talking with staff about what they most value in recognition, and what this might look like as a corporate recognition program, is one of the best ways to protect against negative unintended consequences. Think through the options and try to play out various scenarios. As we will discuss later in the chapter, *by being clear on the why of corporate recognition, the how and the what will fall into place naturally.* Consequences unrelated to intention happen when we think of *what* and *how* and lose sight of the *why*.

Recognition Is **Everyone's** Opportunity and Responsibility

As discussed in earlier chapters, recognition is not simply the job of human resources or organizational development departments or of leadership-at-large. We have also highlighted that *almost every employee wants recognition from their direct supervisor, and that friendship and connection are essential in the workplace. Recognition from peers, therefore, is fundamental in strong recognition cultures.*

Busy CEOs reading this book will be relieved to hear that the best and most meaningful recognition doesn't come from them (although you're not off the hook...you do have direct reports; just imagine the exponential energy produced by a note or call from the CEO). The powerful question for an organization, however, is how to support and enable recognition for and by everyone. Much of the content of previous chapters has been building to this very question.

A common misperception is that the goal is to treat people the way we want to be treated. This Golden Rule is a great place to start, but what if we don't believe recognition of one another is that important? What happens if we believe the paycheque we get is enough recognition? This is why we promote the Platinum Rule, which is to treat people the way *they* want to be treated. This is not simply an altruistic gesture. We get a lot out of doing this right. The benefit and payoff is that the organization evolves; the data tell us a recognition culture fosters innovation, continuous improvement, collaboration, and retention.

1. Staff-to-Staff Recognition

Encouraging staff to recognize one another can become part of the fabric of organizational life. How does an organization recognize something working in one area and between some or all of the staff on a team? How can staff be encouraged to "resource gossip" about their colleagues beyond the walls of their teams? Decision Toolbox publishes recognition from one staff to another in their internal newsletter. In an organization we worked for, we fed the CEO great stories people had shared about their colleagues in workshops so he could surprise people by acknowledging something specific at quarterly all-staff meetings (a great example of exponential energy).

In a nutshell, the goal is to intentionally look for meaningful recognition between staff and explore with them the importance of sharing that positive energy with people who haven't been lucky enough to learn of it. Organizations build trust when their motives for building a strong recognition culture of talent are authentic. Facilitating staff-to-staff recognition is a great example of this. Showcasing recognition that happens when no one is watching makes it clear there isn't an agenda for the act of recognition but that it is a gesture of genuine humanity.

2. Leaders Recognizing Staff (and Vice Versa)

Leaders who make a purposeful effort to learn their staff's areas of greatness and acknowledge them any time an opportunity presents itself build trust and connection, two key ingredients in healthy organizations. Starting on day one, a new leader of a team can spend time getting to know staff as people, what their roles entail, what they like about their jobs, what a good day looks like for them, the most important projects they're working on, and what they're most excited about. Conversely, when new staff join a team, spending time orienting them, explaining what is expected, connecting them with a staff mentor (based on fit), and learning a little more about their talents, passions, and virtues not only will enable them to be more successful but also will affirm for them their good decision to join the organization. It's never too early to work on that retention strategy.

When the two of us became leaders, we learned that we inherited a lot of untapped talent. We saw no point in perpetuating an environment in which people brought only a fraction of their talents, passions, and virtues to work; furthermore, we knew we needed to facilitate a collective opportunity in which the potential of the team was maximized by combining everyone's greatness. Our mandates were larger than what we could accomplish on our own; we needed individuals to bring their collective greatness to the job every day.

The question became how we could motivate people to venture out of their pattern of giving only so much of themselves and working within the narrow confines of their role. After all, as much as the status quo was not ideal, it was comfortable.

What did we do? We asked questions like: What made you choose to join the organization, your field, this team? What work do you most love to do? If you could do more of something or change one thing, what would it be? Sometimes leaders don't ask because they are afraid of the answer. Really, what's the worst that could happen? Staff might say they don't care? Some do care – most, in fact. Quickly for some and slowly for others, staff will see their leader as genuinely caring about them and as trying to find meaningful opportunities for them to do their best work.

Through one-on-one conversations to better understand our staff's greatness, and how they most liked to be recognized, we not only understood better what made our teams tick but also began to prove we were invested in seeing them leverage their talents, passions, and virtues. Sarah uses a tool she picked up from the book *The Baptist Health Care Journey to Excellence: Creating a Culture that WOWs!* in which individuals complete a form that has employees explicitly rate the types of recognition most important to them as well as other fun details such as the way they take their coffee or tea and their favourite pizza toppings. These forms were always within arm's reach.

Time and time again, when Sarah used a strategy to specifically recognize someone in the way they most wanted to be recognized, it had the biggest impact – for example, a private word of praise combined with tea made exactly how they liked it.

Here are some quick and simple questions to elicit conversations of greatness to fuel recognition:

- What do you love about your job?
- If you could spend most of your time doing a particular part of your job, what would it be?
- What do your fellow team members lean on you for?
- Describe your best day to me. What would you have done and how would you feel at the end of it?
- What has been your greatest work accomplishment and why?
- What have you learned about something that didn't work? If you had a "do over," what would you do the same and what would you do differently?
- What have you always been passionate about? When have you been able to live into this passion? What was that like for you?
- What have you become passionate about more recently? Where has this come about and why?
- What have you learned about yourself?

- If you were the teacher and I were the student, what would you teach me?

Leaders are human, too. When employees begin to acknowledge the greatness in the person they report to and in others with supervisory responsibilities, this is a sure sign of momentum. It can't be forced. Most staff do not think it's their role to recognize their direct supervisor. Until they feel they are consistently supported, understood, appreciated, and valued, they will focus on the many other aspects of their work that demand their explicit and discretionary attention.

3. Organizations Recognizing Clients

Some organizations don't stop at internal recognition. They reinforce their recognition culture by recognizing *clients* for their contributions toward the organization's overall success, such as recommending them to prospective clients or soliciting their advice for improvements to a process. This is a unique and important example of full-circle organizational recognition. Seem backwards? We usually see it as *we are helping them*, right? Yes, and they may also help us. Don't we always learn from the new challenges our clients bring to us and from the opportunity to grow organizationally because we have their business?

Let's be honest, we all like working with some clients more than others. Not just because they pay on time. They trust us. They pass our name on to other people looking for our services. They get back to us right away. They do what they say they're going to do. How do we repay this? Perhaps with a corporate "Season's Greetings" card? What more could we be doing? And we don't mean sending them more swag at holiday time.

This is where our learning from Decision Toolbox (DT) continues. DT may do the recruiting for clients, but occasionally their clients recruit new clients to DT. If a lead turns out to be successful, DT gives the client a reward. Some might call this bad business (why are you giving away your profits?). Many of us likely have just never have thought of it. DT has found clients are significantly more loyal *after* they have been rewarded for their part in DT's business success. And the gains are not just financial on both sides.

As Kim says, "So few people in the service industry thank their clients for being human and kind, not just for their business. Acknowledging the worth of kindness I think is really important. They become more loyal likely because they didn't expect to be rewarded, which is as noteworthy as the acknowledgement itself."

The first time you find a meaningful way to acknowledge a client's value, they likely won't expect it. That's why it creates…you guessed it, exponential energy. If part of your purpose as an organization is customer service, recognizing your clients in ways they least expect it will reinforce the sincerity behind that purpose.

Getting Going: Organization-Wide Recognition That FROGs

In his bestselling book *Start with Why*, Simon Sinek describes how organizations often miss the mark by starting with *what* and *how* vs. what is most important: the *why*, or true purpose. By failing to focus on *why*, the heart of what Sinek describes as the "golden circle," organizations waste energy trying to convince staff and customers of the importance of a product, service, or initiative. Any energy gained is usually through manipulation rather than inspiration, which means the success will not be sustainable.

This is a great framework for thinking about what is missing in how organizations tackle recognition (that's right, *tackle* – as if it's a difficult task rather than a way to reinforce the core purpose of the business). They emphasize the planning and execution of the *what*. Assuming there ever was a *why* to begin with, many recognition programs no longer exemplify it.

For example, we might say this about a recognition program:

- What: Employee-of-the-Month Program
- How: Manager hangs picture of Employee of the Month on the wall for all to see
- Why: So customers see we care about our staff and the employee feels good

What if someone doesn't want his picture hung on the wall? What if he prefers a personalized thank you and, because his boss hung up a picture, he thinks he's done his job for the month (*"My work here is done"*)? What if the customers, let alone the employees, believe the intention behind the Employee of the Month is not genuine? Or what if it had meaning at first and now feels like it's just on a rotation? What if no one believes the way people are chosen for the award is fair? Because the focus is on the *what*, the *why* gets lost. *The why is bound up in what effective recognition is: the genuine appreciation and acknowledgement of greatness.*

It is no wonder programs like these have little to no positive impact – certainly not in terms of return on time or financial investment.

Let's try this again, starting with *why*, and see where we end up:

- Why: Staff are motivated to do their best work because they feel genuinely appreciated for the value they bring
- How: Anyone can nominate a colleague, subordinate, or supervisor who has gone above and beyond by sharing a specific example of something the person did the month before
- What: A verbal or written thank you and publication in the company newsletter of stories of those going above and beyond

What you do is secondary to why you do it. When your recognition activities are grounded in a solid *why*, they are more likely to resonate with those who deserve acknowledgement. As a result, anyone can feel good when that award is handed out, not just the person receiving it. We certainly don't want to perpetuate a sense of competition.

Let's look at how the company we profiled earlier, Decision Toolbox, demonstrates this approach.

1. The *Why*	2. The *How*	3. The *What*
We focus on strengths rather than deficits, enabling our best work.	Walk around and look for people doing great work. Write it down and submit to leaders.	"Attaboy" monthly award.
Goodwill among colleagues gets everyone farther than competition.	Have colleagues submit examples when they have "caught" someone doing something great.	"Caught in the Act" newsletter acknowledgements.
People are people first, with many talents and interests. They want to share them with their co-workers.	Invite employees to present or lead co-workers through a personal talent or interest (e.g., yoga, nutrition lecture).	Me, We, Inc. Annual All-Staff Meeting.
You can learn from seeing failures as a teaching opportunity (so don't be afraid to mess up).	Share publicly during weekly staff meetings, in a blame-free environment, examples of situations that went wrong, including if an employee did something he/she shouldn't have.	"Biggest Oops" Award.

People will want to work for a culture that values their humanity, believes they have talents and passions worth sharing, and knows they will learn more by messing up (and sharing this learning with others).

Getting Focused

We hope you're ready to gather a cross-section of people committed to looking hard at your corporate recognition methods – at what is and is not working. We know it's important to have support for doing this, so why not start with finding out who among staff, middle managers, and senior leadership wants to be part of this exploration? As shown in this chapter, some key first steps will be to:

- Collect data
- Get out of the office: talk with people, observe, and ask questions
- Get real about what's working
- Gather ideas of different ways or new ways to recognize people
- Dive deep to understand how teams have built strong co-worker recognition
- Study leaders whose staff are most satisfied so you can help other leaders

Next comes building a compelling case for why improved recognition will help shift the culture. More to the point, it is about posing to the organization *the importance of building a culture in which the people who add value are able to bring their greatness to work every day because they know it is needed and appreciated.*

Closing Reflection

Ready? Jump in!

Suppose it is six months from now, and there has been a shift in your organization's culture. People are being recognized regularly for their unique talents, passions, and virtues. This is noticeable at the organizational level. Individuals and teams are highly engaged.

- *What is the first thing you notice when you walk in to work that tells you something must have happened in the last six months?*
- *What are your colleagues noticing and saying?*
- *What are the clients noticing and saying?*

- What else?
- What are you able to do now that you weren't able to before?
- What do you want to do next?
- What difference will that make?

Inspiration for Action

Surprise is the best recognition there is. I think surprise trumps money. It takes forethought. Surprises take unsurprising planning by somebody. A surprise doesn't cost anything.

–Kim Shepherd

If you want someone to do a good job, give them a good job to do.

–Frederick Herzberg

Take the time to build exponential energy into your recognition events. It's worth every minute of planning because the buzz will last long after the event is over!

–Kim Shepherd

That some achieve great success, is proof to all that others can achieve it as well.

–Abraham Lincoln

Leaders, I have to caution you. You have to make recognition part of your job description. It doesn't just happen by the seat of your pants. It takes critical thinking. We have a tendency to think critical thinking goes to business things, but it goes to "purpose things" really – this is not just the extracurricular.

–Kim Shepherd

All leadership is appreciative leadership. It's the capacity to see the best in the world around us, in our colleagues, and in the groups we are trying to lead.

–David Cooperrider

This is not about me as CEO. It takes a collection of people to make any organization great.

–Stuart MacLeod

Six

Manage Change with Resiliency:
A FROG for Every Season

Opening Reflection

This chapter focuses on one of the most dominant themes in organizations today: managing and thriving through change. A key ingredient to successful change is resiliency, and, you guessed it, recognition is a fundamental resiliency booster in times of change.

We encourage you to consider new concepts in this chapter to ensure change leads to the outcomes you want – for yourself, your colleagues, and the larger group – with respect to a change you are currently leading or part of. These concepts apply to situations across the spectrum, from going well to going off the rails.

Reflecting on your strengths and resources, what do you know is already working well? What is already helping to make the change a success (however you define that – for yourself, for others, or for the greater good)? What are you doing to contribute to that?

On a scale of 10 to 1, with 10 standing for **"I am completely confident I am doing what I need to do in order to ensure successful change"** and 1 being the opposite of that, where are you now? Where would you like to be? Imagine you are one step higher. What are you doing differently?

10	9	8	7	6	5	4	3	2	1

Now imagine you have finished reading this chapter and have succeeded in doing or adjusting something that took you one step higher. How will you know what you tried is having an impact? What does that impact look like for others, you, and the change itself?

One of the most resourceful strategies at everyone's disposal, regardless of the scope or type of change, is to engage the hearts, not just the minds, of those involved in and affected by a change. We're not the first to make such a statement. From change guru Kotter to transitions expert Bridges, time and time again we're reminded change will take longer and may even fail to achieve the desired results unless people are engaged throughout – with their fears, their questions, their ideas, and so forth. This chapter explores the essential role of recognition in successful change.

Noticing Greatness in Times of Change

We worked for several years with an organization that underwent significant change – *transformational* change. It was a publicly funded organization in an industry that, until the 1990s, saw its share of clinician-driven advancements that improved the outcomes of those it served but did so with little externally inflicted change. All of a sudden, major changes were required internally because of significant external factors: fiscal constraints, new regulations, technological advances, and workforce shortages. And the pace of change seemed to gain momentum every year.

We worked with this organization from mid-2000 into the next decade. New senior leaders and a turnover of middle managers brought a new focus on challenging the status quo, having difficult conversations, and being innovative. Technology became an intimate part of everyday work processes, initially causing stress to many providers who rarely used a computer. Continuous quality improvement through LEAN was introduced, requiring people to look for and value surfacing problems and opportunities after decades in which they had learned to live with what frustrated them and had been discouraged from raising issues. New roles were introduced, team members' roles were reconfigured, and the way people practiced was changed. That's not all. Also in the air were deficit-reduction activities and possible integrations or partnerships with other organizations. Is it any wonder all this culminated in a significant dip in morale?

Recognition is all the more important in situations like this. In looking back at all the ways we helped those who led, influenced, or supported the change, there is one important strategy we wish had been attended to: giving staff and leaders sufficient time to honour the past, recognizing what was already working that could be brought in to the present and future, and making sure people felt their talents, passions, and virtues were honoured and valued.

In challenging times, it is easy to become so focused on the projects we're involved in that we forget about the little things. This is especially so for leaders. The people going through the change, however, become hyper alert to the little things. The challenge for leaders is not only to plan the change but also to be sensitive to how each decision and action is going to be examined for clues as to what is going on, what people can expect, and how trustworthy leaders are. All too often, the people leading change are focused on a beautiful vision of the future state while the people who have to make it happen are struggling through present realities and new expectations.

Let's look at four key steps to ensure successful transformation:

1. Jump in to the pond to get sticky

2. Honour greatness

3. Call on all influencers to set up a greatness ripple effect

4. Focus on mindset, attitudes, and communication

1. Jump in to the Pond to Get Sticky

To support the change, we must support the people – which can happen only if we're out there with them. That's the first part of "getting sticky." Although people may question our intentions at first, may be leery of having us around, and may hold back information, the more we get out of our office or cubicle and in to the environment with people, the more they will realize we genuinely want to incorporate the things they do and value into the *what* and *how* of the change.

People are fond nowadays of saying, *"It's important not to lose sight of the big picture"* and *"Don't get stuck in the weeds."* However, we're not aware of any successful transformation that was executed by leaders at a distance. *Change succeeds when change agents jump in to the pond and wade through to understand the most important parts of the environment from those who work and live in it.* It's not easy; we get it. It takes a lot of time. It takes courage. However, by being present in this way, leaders learn how people feel about a lot of things, not just the change: what they like and don't like, what is working and what frustrates them, the people they trust and those they don't.

We need to have the courage to speak genuinely as opposed to just using the key messages given to us. We need to address what people need to hear or understand at that moment based on what they are most passionate about. We also can't be there just for our own benefit – to learn what we can and leave – because that's a recipe for not learning much. Instead of just deciding what we're going to attend to, *we need to let those in the environment determine what we need to understand.* This is what will give us a true and holistic picture.

How Sticky Are Change Agents?

Thinking of a recent or current change:
- *To what extent did those driving the change spend time in the work environment impacted most by the change?*
- *What could be better understood by spending more time or time differently in gemba?*
- *Are those who add value considered essential partners in planning the change?*

Going to Gemba ("Go and See")

In the LEAN continuous improvement world, the Japanese word "gemba" means "the real or actual place." It is where the value is created – on the operating table, at the checkout counter, in the classroom. Gemba is where leaders and change agents "go and see" and therefore need to be comfortable spending their time to truly understand the business they're trying to influence.

The power of gemba is in maintaining an open, curious mind and being non-directive.

Disciplined leaders who practice gemba can stand in a gemba circle for hours, just observing every minute detail of the environment. On another day, they may ask lots of questions and provide lots of compliments, ultimately respecting that the person doing the work is the most important teacher in that moment.

The payoff of the gemba approach is the ability it gives us to make more informed plans, bringing people along with us rather than doing change to them.

2. Honour Greatness When We See It

"Getting sticky" involves noticing small and large examples of greatness at work. The sooner and more authentically we recognize them, the more credibility we will have when we move beyond observation to working with teams to change things that aren't working.

Recognition is the glue that keeps change agents grounded in the present. *To understand how to best create the new world, we need to find concrete ways to honour the past and current state.* Who are the historians who can share some of the most notable stories from the past? Who are the social conveners who keep traditions alive? What gets celebrated and how? What stories, rituals, symbols, or traditions can be used to bridge past and future? The process of learning these things communicates that the need for change is not a result of poor-quality work or bad people, nor is the change more important than the work or the people. A sure-fire way to get people to adopt the change rather than resist it is to understand and value them.

We sometimes hear this from change agents: *"The change is already big enough. Why do I have to pull people along as well as try to move mountains?"* Well, the reality is, change doesn't happen in a vacuum; we have to help people anyway, so why not begin with what they're most passionate about, where their strengths are, and what they value most? If we meet them where they're at, they'll be more likely to travel the rest of the journey *with* us.

Greatness Croaking

Most people think frogs croak more at night. In fact, they croak all day long. It makes sense: it's part of their hardwiring for survival. It's just that we're able to hear them better when the rest of the environment is quieter. *The lesson:* In busy, noisy environments, we don't hear the greatness "croaking." We need to stop to listen. We have to attend to greatness in order to hear it.

It takes seconds to observe greatness and a minute to acknowledge it in the moment. The effect, however, lasts well beyond this brief investment of time and energy. Why not try it out? See if, as a result, the people recognized demonstrate increased:

- Self-regard
- Motivation to do more of what was recognized
- Positive affect
- Attempts to recognize others
- Willingness to engage in discussion and solution-finding

What's the worst that could happen? Whatever it may be, these potential gains suggest it's worth the risk.

3. Call on All Influencers to Set Up a Greatness Ripple Effect

The bestselling book *Influencer: The Power to Change Anything* presents a model of influence that, in a nutshell, attests to the lasting change created when we influence both *ability* and *motivation*. But the point we're interested most in here is that this can be done at an individual, team, and organizational level to create a greatness ripple effect.

FROGing to Influence Others to Use Recognition During Change

As we were getting sticky and noticing greatness in our consulting work, we tried to FROG as many individuals and groups as we could. We complimented people when they did something outstanding. We pointed out the gains the team made, however large or small. We coached leaders one-on-one, always acknowledging and helping them recognize gains they were making. We took every opportunity to positively influence anyone we could whenever we could. As we saw close up and personal, this strategy is very helpful when many changes are happening at once across an organization.

As John Izzo proposes in his book *Stepping Up: How Taking Responsibility Changes Everything,* all we need to focus on is influencing those in our circle in a meaningful way, because this alone will cause a sufficient ripple effect. The people we influence will in turn impact those in their circles, and the ripple will continue to widen. We not only are more motivated to influence those closest to us, but we also are less likely to question our ability to do so.

For transformation to take root, the FROG process needs to be practiced by a critical mass of influencers, both formally and informally. The breadth and spread must be farther and faster than what a few people can do alone, no matter what role those individuals may have in the organization. That's the beauty of recognition: everyone can be an influencer wherever they are in the organization. Spreading the influencing around helps keep the vital few from burning out. (See the next chapter for a discussion of compassion satisfaction vs. compassion fatigue.)

4. Focus on Mindset, Attitudes, and Communication

Our next point is obvious, but it's so important we want to say it anyway. Mindset, our established set of attitudes, matters even more in times of change. Our first step, therefore, is to ask individuals what talents, passions, and virtues they have to offer. The next is to ensure we reinforce a meaningful connection through our attention and tone of voice. Let's look at mindset, attitudes, and communication during times of change.

Mindset and attitudes matter all the more when we're not at our best, which may be the case during change. Our true views and opinions come out when we're confronted with questions we don't know the answers to or don't want to answer, when people push back or push our buttons, or when we're tired and stressed. In these moments we forget our onstage face and operate from our default views. In these moments people could lose faith in the change and its leaders, perhaps to the extent that it's difficult to earn it back. If the people we expect to accept the change don't value those who are leading them through it and don't believe in their abilities, this may lead to a feeling of hopelessness in the present and for the future. If those going through the change are not managing their own stress levels and frustrations well and don't feel safe to tell the truth, they may read through even the most scripted of messages delivered with all the right words and come to their own conclusions.

We can say all the right things, but, as every communication textbook tells us, what people believe is predominantly based on our tone of voice and facial expressions, not on the words we use. People intuitively know we can practice what we want to say but our non-verbal cues give away whether we mean what we're saying. *When we truly believe something from the past is worth bringing forward, traditions are worth honouring, and successes are worth celebrating, it will be reflected in how our words match our body language.*

Reconnecting to What Works

Think of a difficult change you went through, one you thought you might not make it through. Perhaps it was the loss of a job, a divorce, or an illness. Looking back at how you survived, think about how this has impacted you today, perhaps making you even better. Reflect on your own or with a friend and create a list of strategies for yourself based on the answers to these questions:

- *What helped?*
- *What else? (ask this five more times...trust us)*
- *Who helped?*
- *Who else?*

FROG Metamorphosis Questions

Change can feel overwhelming, so we may find it comforting to understand that change happens one step at a time. We only need to determine what the most important first step is. Much like a team's metamorphosis (explored in chapter four, "Enable Greatness with Healthy Team Ecosystems"), change can also be likened to the natural cycle of evolution. The steps can't be rushed. Honouring each step, guiding and supporting it through, ensures a natural progression.

FROG – Forever Recognize Others Greatness™

Here are examples of FROG metamorphosis questions to ask during times of change:

1. The Beginning (egg)

   - What talents, passions, and virtues will enable you to accomplish your goal?
   - What might the positive effect be?

2. Planning for the Future (tadpole)

   - Suppose a miracle happens while you're sleeping and the change has already occurred smoothly. What's the first thing you'll notice in the morning to tell you things are better?
   - Who will be the first person to notice that things are different for you without your saying anything?

3. Already Working (froglet)

   - What are one or more things that have already occurred in your miracle?
   - How did you specifically contribute to this?

4. Checking Progress (new frog)

   - On a scale of 10 to 1, with 10 standing for your desired outcome and 1 being the opposite of that, where are you right now?
   - What tells you you're at that number and not any lower?

5. Actioning (mature frog)

   - What and who could give you confidence along the way?
   - What will be your first step?

You may have already identified, through reading this chapter, what you feel should be your next step. To assist you, let's quickly recap salient points on how to recognize the greatness in others to ensure change is successful:

1. Make a commitment to recognize greatness as much as possible.
   - *How could you try this or augment what you're already doing?*

2. Every day, spend time where the work happens, understanding it from the perspective of those who add value.
   - *How could you shift time from activities that do not support change to make room for the time and energy to be more present?*

3. Set a goal for how many times you would like to acknowledge greatness.
   - *What goal might you set?*
   - *What will success look like when you achieve this?*

4. Try out different recognition approaches that feel authentic for you (gauge the reaction of others to see how well they're working).
   - *What recognition approach has worked for you in the past that you would like to do more of or start using again?*

5. Every day, acknowledge for yourself at least one way you made a positive impact on someone or something through recognition.
   - *How could you ritualize acknowledgement of self or others?*
   - *How can you build this into your resiliency toolkit to maintain your compassion satisfaction and protect against compassion fatigue?*
   - *How could you be held accountable until this behaviour becomes a habit?*

Closing Reflection

Bolstering Success

Thinking of a change that needs to be successful, consider how you can incorporate recognition to bolster the likelihood of success.

- *How do you already leverage recognition? What is already working?*

- *How could you make recognition an even greater priority?*

- *What will people involved in the change say and do that will indicate they feel their talents, passions, and virtues are being honoured and leveraged during the change?*

- *What impact will this have on the change?*

Inspiration for **Action**

Never miss an opportunity to celebrate and elevate another person.

–Robin Sharma

If you change the way you look at things, the things you look at change.

–Wayne Dyer

Learn from the people. Plan with the people. Begin with what they have. Build on what they know. Of the best leaders, when the task is accomplished, the people will remark, we have done it ourselves.

–Lao-Tzu

If you don't like something, change it. If you can't change it, change your attitude.

–Maya Angelou

Sometimes it's the smallest decision that can change your life forever.

–Keri Russell

Be the change you want to see in the world.

–Mohandas Gandhi

When you dance, your purpose is not to get to a certain place on the dance floor. It's to enjoy each step along the way.

–Wayne Dyer

Seven

LeapFROG Your Way Through Roadblocks

Opening Reflection

This chapter explores the roadblocks that can stand in the way of personal, team, and organizational greatness. Fortunately, we have many strategies to offer you, demonstrating how recognition is a key tool to unblock you and your team or organization when you are struggling.

Think of a personal or team roadblock currently in the way of maximizing performance and satisfaction. What is the roadblock? What impact is it having on you or others?

Now imagine you get up tomorrow morning from the most restful sleep you have ever had. As you begin to go through your day, you notice that somehow the roadblock is no longer there. What tipped you off to its disappearance? How do you feel? What is your energy like? What are you doing differently? How is your thinking different? What could you try now that you would not have tried had the roadblock still been present?

Now, on a scale of 10 to 1, with 10 standing for **"I have successfully addressed the roadblock"** and 1 being the opposite of that, where are you now?

| 10 | 9 | 8 | 7 | 6 | 5 | 4 | 3 | 2 | 1 |

Where would you like to be? Imagine you are one step higher. What would you be looking for in this chapter that might give you insight to help you get there? When you realize this insight, what will you do next? What will you do to maintain momentum to reach the next step on the scale?

We don't want you to get frustrated in your efforts to use FROG and other strategies to recognize greatness in your interpersonal relationships, on teams, and throughout your organization. There will always be roadblocks. This chapter focuses on some we see most often, how you can catch them early, and what you can do to turn them into opportunities.

Let's start with Lana's story.

Lana was a senior director of a small not-for-profit agency serving the most vulnerable people in her community. She was passionate that all clients and families would have a good experience when using the agency's services. She worked hard to bridge service gaps and improve quality. Problem was, she was burnt out. The teams she managed were struggling. The programs expanded faster than new staff and supervisors could be brought on. Wait lists grew. Accreditation standards were not being consistently met, and policies were outdated.

Lana felt she needed to get a handle on so many aspects of what she was responsible for, and, despite prioritizing to-do lists, she found by Friday of each week she was fatigued, frustrated, and disappointed, with not one important item crossed off the list. She could see her supervisors and managers were experiencing the same strain and didn't have time to coach them or properly check in with them.

She worked from six a.m. to eight p.m. six days a week and didn't see any progress. She began wondering if she could do the job, if her colleagues thought she was competent enough for it, or if she even wanted to do it anymore.

The tricky thing about roadblocks is that they can build to the point of feeling insurmountable and permanent. Remember the boiling frog reference from chapter four? What we choose to ignore today may build to a point that it stands in our way tomorrow, preventing us from asserting ourselves to work through interpersonal tensions and challenge negative self-talk. We blindly accept assumptions as facts.

Drawing on our work with individuals, teams, and organizations, we have come up with a list of common roadblocks. Keep in mind here that, although we have experienced all of these at one time or another, there were countless times when we didn't. *We hope you'll attend equally to such exceptions in your own experience. The exceptions, the times when the problem doesn't exist, can remind you of the talents, passions, and virtues to draw on when roadblocks do present themselves.* Common roadblocks:

1. Negative inner critic.

2. Compassion fatigue.

3. The blame game.

4. Untrue assumptions.

5. Guilt, envy, and other unhelpful emotions.

6. Fear of conflict.

7. Avoidance of challenging conversations.

No one is immune to these roadblocks. Fortunately, there are lots of strategies for working through them and even more successes that have already worked for most of us.

What Roadblock Are You Working Through?

In reading this list of roadblocks, does one of them already stand out for you? What aspects of this chapter do you most need to direct your energy and attention to so you can tap back in to your talents, passions, and virtues? Who in your life has experienced a similar roadblock, and what can you learn from how they overcame it? Was there a time when you experienced something similar to this roadblock? What did you do to overcome it? How can you apply these reflections to the rest of the chapter?

Negative Inner Critic

We all have an inner voice that croaks a litany of unhelpful comments at the most inopportune times, whether in a job interview (*"You're not qualified"*), with colleagues (*"Look at them compared with you...you're not smart/experienced/creative enough to be here"*), during a meeting (*"No one wants to hear what you have to say"*), or during a presentation (*"This is not going well – who are you trying to kid?"*). Any of these sound familiar? You will have your own series of internal comments, likely harsher than anything you would say to someone else. So why does this running commentary prevail in our heads?

Believe it or not, the inner critic can be helpful; the critic's job is to alert us to something we need to pay attention to. The tricky thing is that the inner critic has the maturity of a seven-year-old. Would you take professional and life advice from your primary school neighbour (as if she would even say something so cruel)? No, she hasn't experienced enough of life to advise you on what to stay to a prospective boss, how to be respected by your peers, and sure-fire methods to wow people in meetings or presentations. In other words, it's not *what* the inner critic is saying but the fact it's *showing up* that matters. Therefore, the two most important questions in these situations are:

1. Why has the inner critic shown up now?

2. What do I need to notice that I'm not currently aware of?

As soon as we see the inner critic as an insightful trigger rather than an informant, we can move past the roadblock of the negative unhelpful message to look for the resourceful opportunity that may be revealed when we respond to what the inner critic is saying. Connecting to how the critic serves us is important in order to fend off what we described in chapter three as the impostor syndrome. If you let your inner critic get the better of you, you can find yourself stalled in making decisions, not trusting your instincts, or generally just not following a path that enables you to practice your talents, passions, and virtues to the fullest. Some healthy humility is great; what we're talking about, however, are times when we take our self-effacing qualities to the extreme.

What's Up, Critic?

When we're coaching and a client is preoccupied with negative thoughts and perceived barriers rather than possibilities, we suggest their inner critic could be interfering. Here are some things to explore when the inner critic pipes up:

1. What specific statements is the inner critic making?

2. When does the inner critic show up? What are the triggers or connections?

3. Of the possible reasons the inner critic is showing up, which seems most likely? How could this be tested?

4. If you put aside the specific things the inner critic says and you believe for a second it was here to serve you, what service might it be offering? What might it be alerting you to?

5. If the inner critic were able to make a suggestion in a mature and resourceful way, what might that be?

6. Suppose your inner critic were able to offer a suggestion beginning with, *"I'm wondering..."* What might that be? Thinking of all of your strengths and resources, what would you like to try? What would you expect would happen to the inner critic once you have tried this? What do you already know that works?

Helping Lana, #1

Where do you think Lana's inner critic might be showing up? What insight might it be trying to alert her to? Thinking about this insight, if you were to reinforce her most resourceful self by FROGing her (recognizing her greatness), what might you say? How might this open up a dialogue for her to talk about exceptions and reconnect with her strengths? How could you help her see how her inner critic is serving her and then shift her attention to exploring resourceful strategies and options?

Strategies for Moving Past Our Inner Critic's Monologues

As we have been suggesting, it's important to find ways to move past the actual negative and unhelpful inner critic statements. Here are some suggestions.

1. Practice the steps above under, "What's Up, Critic?"

2. Practice self-resource gossiping. As we have discussed earlier in this book, resource gossiping is a healthy way to encourage dialogue about what is working rather than what is not. If the inner critic is showing up when you're delivering a presentation, ask yourself what your best friend might say are all the things she knows you already do well and the areas where you've already improved.

3. Practice thankfulness. When you thank the inner critic for its role in getting you to understand a core message, you give it less of a role to play. Yes, that's right, we're actually suggesting you FROG your inner critic!

Try these and other strategies that work for you and we guarantee, even though you may not hear it, a voice in the distance will be saying, *"Okay, my job here is done. I'm going outside to play now!"*

Compassion Fatigue

Sometimes we find it hard to be resourceful when we have given so much of ourselves that we have little energy, time, or compassion left. People who work as professional healers, frontline service personnel, full-time caregivers, teachers, managers, and customer service representatives, giving more of themselves than perhaps they get in return to recharge their batteries, are at risk of something called compassion fatigue.

Renowned compassion fatigue expert Françoise Mathieu points out that this kind of fatigue is a normal consequence of doing a good job; if people didn't care about the work they did or the people they worked with, they wouldn't be at risk of feeling emotionally fatigued. *In other words, what juices us, giving us life and passion for our work, can also cause our downfall if we don't regularly check in with what we need to fuel ourselves.*

We are following many newcomers to this field who are beginning to examine the topic of compassion fatigue through a solution-focused lens, looking for compassion satisfaction and vicarious resilience, studying what allows certain people to retain their sense of hope, empathy, optimism, and energy. For our purposes, we choose to believe we all start from a strong positive place.

Three stages of compassion fatigue are often described in the literature, which we build on here using the stoplight metaphor of green for recognizing greatness, yellow for resisting greatness, and red for resenting greatness.

Green: Recognizing Greatness

When we're most resourceful, we're in a state of compassion satisfaction. We feel balanced and healthy. We're able to notice and recognize the greatness in others, which may become part of what we do, how we think, and how we act. We energize throughout the day; we may get tired, but we experience it as the normal result of a long day of a job well done. We're able to recharge with the things we enjoy and find time to fit them in, whether it is family time, spiritual practices, or leisure activities. Engaging in these activities and others throughout the day gives us a feeling of fulfillment, excitement, inspiration, and encouragement. This is where our most resourceful FROGing happens.

Yellow: Resisting Greatness – Missed Opportunities to Leverage Greatness

There are warning signs that we're shifting from compassion satisfaction to the early stages of compassion fatigue, important cues that something is out of balance and we need to pay attention to how to regain that balance. We may be neglecting the things that fuel and recharge us, or these things may not be giving us the boost they normally do. We may be more focused on what's not working than on what is, in ourselves and with others at work. We move away from seeing the long-term possibilities of situations and relationships, becoming more narrow and short-term in our focus and choices.

The longer we ignore these cues, the more likely we are to transition to red. After all, these signs are gentle warnings that we're at a turning point. Will we move toward compassion satisfaction by re-engaging in all the practices we know work best for us or grind to a halt in the face of harder times to come?

Red: Resenting Greatness

By the time we're in the red, we're frustrated, defensive, and discouraged. Natural gifts, such as problem-solving, solution-building, and critical thinking, may come across to others as difficult and argumentative behaviours.

We may feel helpless to improve the situation, particularly if it's been a long time building to this point. Often we're disconnected from the things we're passionate about, not spending time in activities and with people who refuel us. In fact, we may turn to self-soothing strategies that are actually destructive, such as gossip, self-isolation, and sometimes even substances. This can be linked to a sense of disengagement, not only with the people and environments we live or work in but also with our authentic self. We fail to see our own greatness, and, from this less resourceful place, we also have less energy or desire to look for it, let alone acknowledge it in others. As with coloured frogs in nature, bright red stands for poison and danger.

Staying in this state of compassion fatigue for extended periods of time can negatively impact our relationships, health, well-being, and confidence. Any greatness in us that is noticed causes us to be defensive; we reject it outwardly or allow it to continue chipping away at our confidence inwardly.

Compassion Fatigue Quick Diagnostic Tool

The following behaviours and emotions are associated with the three stages of compassion fatigue. This quick reference will help you see if there is an issue worth digging in to in yourself or others and to encourage you to do what works to stay green.*

	Physical Signs and Symptoms	Behavioural Signs and Symptoms	Psychological Signs and Symptoms
Green Frog	Energetic Healthy Normal appetite	Balance of work and life Enjoying work and satisfied with results Social Creative and innovative	Happy Contented Hopeful Optimistic
Yellow Frog	Fatigued Waking not feeling rested Decreasing energy during the day Change in appetite and physical health regimens	Working through lunch and breaks Avoiding social interactions Behaving in opposite ways to the norm Acting on feelings of envy and jealousy Irritable	Less interested in friendships Distancing Skeptical Less hopeful Teary Hard to please Reduced ability to feel sympathy and empathy
Red Frog	Exhaustion Insomnia Headaches Increased susceptibility to illness Extreme changes in appetite	Difficulty separating personal and professional lives Soothing through substances Absenteeism Anger and irritability Avoidance of important personal and work connections Impaired ability to make decisions Problems in personal relationships Compromised care of self and others Conflict avoidance Failure to nurture and develop non-work-related aspects of life	Emotional exhaustion Reclusive Negative self-image Depressed mood Loss of hope Anxiousness Guilt Inability to feel appropriate sympathy and empathy Cynicism Resentment Dread of being with certain people Professional hopelessness and helplessness Disruption of worldview Heightened anxiety or irrational fears Inability to tolerate strong feelings

* Adapted from sources: Saakvitne (1995), Figley (1995), Gentry, Baranowsky & Dunning (1997), Yassen (1995).

Attending to Our Circle of Influence vs. Circle of Concern

Just as Stephen Covey has taught us, we are concerned about many things we have virtually no control over. An overly heightened focus here will serve only to leave us feeling frustrated and deflated. Asking ourselves what we do have control over, no matter how small, can empower us to act where our influence lies. Even if it's just our beliefs and emotions about a person or situation, we always have control over something.

Helping Lana, #2

Reflecting on the story of Lana at the beginning of this chapter, would you guess she was in the green, yellow, or red phase? What are the signs of the colour you think she's in? What are the signs she could be pulled back to a more resourceful colour? What might a good colleague or friend provide as advice about what she could do to focus on her resources rather than what is not working? How might this help her tackle the challenges of her job by not being weighed down from being in the red?

The good news is no one state is permanent. It's true the longer someone sits in yellow or red, the harder it is to shift to green, but it is far from impossible (though that may be hard to believe at the time). Whether we notice it in ourselves, or we're trying to help an individual or a team notice it, awareness can be sharpened.

Strategies for Overcoming Compassion Fatigue

Here are six ways to combat compassion fatigue while staying in a state of compassion satisfaction.

1. Take stock of what is going on around and inside you. Notice the signs early. Try to notice the signs that green is transitioning to yellow or yellow to red. Simply being aware in this way will shift your attention from what's not working to the choices available to you to operate from a more enjoyable state of compassion satisfaction.

2. Focus on your talents, passions, and virtues. Find a safe and natural outlet to use them consistently. If you're already compassion fatigued at work, don't give more time and energy to work; instead, shift some energy to

things that give you fuel (e.g., volunteering at a soup kitchen, going to yoga, spending more time with close family, friends, pets). Set an intention and commit to one small step to re-energize and refocus on what makes you your best self.

3. Create a self-care list. Review the list of things you know work for you and choose one to include in your day or week. Identify a way to reflect on it and celebrate successes.

4. Tap in to past compliments or words of thanks. If you have kept them, reread them; if you have not, start doing so. Reflect on some of the best compliments you have ever received. Nurture yourself with the words. Let them land; do not dismiss them.

5. Reflect on the question, *"What do I have control over, no matter how small?"* What are your choices and options? Based on this, decide the things you feel compelled to focus on that you can influence. Decide what you will stop focusing on.

6. Think of a time when you were compassion fatigued. What did you do that helped move you from red or yellow to green? What from that experience could you try again?

For more ideas and stories from those who have moved from compassion fatigue back to compassion satisfaction, please visit our websites <www.bzmsolutions.com> and <www.greatnessmagnified.com>.

It goes without saying we are not making medical or therapeutic recommendations here. We can't emphasize enough that experts should be consulted for true, extended periods of compassion fatigue, which may have ripple effects on mental and physical health. Not everyone needs the same type of support, nor is everyone at the point where professional attention is necessary. Tapping in to the right professional help, should it be required, or trialing strategies like the ones listed above, will assist you in moving through this roadblock for both short- and long-term well-being.

The Blame Game

In their bestselling book *Crucial Confrontations*, Patterson, Grenny, McMillan, and Switzler caution us to watch for three clever stories: victim stories (*"It's not my fault"*), villain stories (*"It's all your fault"*), and helpless stories (*"There's nothing else I can do"*). All three are unhelpful because they place blame on ourselves or others or shut down possibilities. They're clever because they make us feel a sense of comfort during very difficult situations, often in our relationships with others. They're all disempowering, however, because they get us stuck in a rut of blame, leaving little room for creativity, possibility-oriented thinking, or action.

In North American hospitals, millions of incidents of harm every year are attributed to communication breakdowns, often linked to a blame culture (e.g., someone didn't speak up about a safety concern to a doctor or nurse out of fear of their reaction). Hard to believe, but some cultures of blame are so strong we find ourselves doing things we would never do if the culture weren't filled with victims and villains. We have no doubt experienced times when we've chosen not to act or speak up because the risk of doing so seemed greater than the gains.

Helping Lana, #3

Lana has been unable to get all the policies up-to-date. Every time she walks in to a meeting she feels someone is going to point this out. When they don't, she believes they're thinking it. Sometimes she gets really angry about this. How could her boss think it's reasonable to give her such a big portfolio? Why don't her colleagues offer to help her? Why don't the supervisors or staff take initiative and revise the policies without her having to ask?

In a meeting in which Lana is experiencing extreme compassion fatigue, she blurts out, "I'm not going to wear it if we don't pass accreditation because none of our policies have been updated!"

What might help her shift her thinking away from blame? How might she feel she is not in this alone? What actions might she or others take to ensure neither she nor they is seen as the villain, and in so doing, the work can get done?

Greatness is suffocated when blame is present because we're spending all our time and energy protecting, deflecting, and worrying. This suffocation can be facilitated by our environment, but we can also manifest it all on our own. It seems counterintuitive. Why would we reinforce something that is unhealthy for us and our relationships? Our instinct to protect ourselves is automatic, and sometimes how we do that actually hurts us in the long term.

This is why recognition is so important. It is the insulation in the walls of our culture. There are no victims and villains in recognition conversations, just people with flaws and fabulousness alike. If we know people value and see our strengths, we're better able to accept responsibility and be forgiven for any errors rather than select a clever story to excuse ourselves. When we do not begin from that level of trust, comfort, and acceptance, we're more likely to shirk responsibility and place blame on other people and situations.

Strategies to Overcome the Blame Game

The following strategies are simply the tip of the iceberg. There are many, and, depending on how deep a blame culture is, an array of strategies may be required.

1. Retrace your path. The book *Crucial Confrontations* offers a helpful strategy: going back to what enabled the unhelpful "clever story" to take root. This will force you to debunk some of the initial inputs that contributed to the clever story. The steps go like this:

   - What did I see/hear?
   - What story did I tell myself?
   - How did it make me feel?
   - What did I do/how did I act as a result?

2. By cycling through these questions (for this must be done a few times), other ways of looking at a situation often become clear. The initial story starring you as the victim and another person as the villain can be replaced with a less dramatic but equally plausible script. Life isn't a Hollywood movie, so why accept a dramatic role when it leaves you with so much less energy to play the other important scenes in your life?

3. Take the Learner rather than Judger Path. Use the question Marilee Adams offers in her Choice Map, described in her book *Change Your Questions, Change Your Life* (you can Google a free download of the map). Simply by shifting your questions from blaming questions to solution-focused questions can open you up to more positive conversations and possibilities.

4. Focus on what is already working, no matter how small. Then, and only then, consider what needs to change or is not working. This applies to inner dialogue and reflection, speaking one-on-one with someone, attending a

meeting, or taking part in a large group setting. This shift in perspective will help you attend to and generate energy instead of getting stuck in a rut.

Untrue Assumptions

Assumptions are tricky things because we're rarely conscious of how many we have and what they are. We can also produce new ones pretty easily. It's an almost automatic process, built in part by our need to quickly and consistently make sense of a complex world. If we didn't make assumptions based on information from the past and our best read of the present, we would spend more time on meaning-making than on the business of living our lives. The challenge is to become more aware of our assumptions to ensure they are accurate and helpful.

As discussed in chapter three, Peter Senge has done a lot of work in this area. His bestselling book *The Fifth Discipline* presents much evidence that what we believe is self-generated and untested. We believe:

- The truth of our beliefs is obvious
- Our beliefs are based on real data
- The data we select are real

Challenging these assumptions, therefore, is no easy task.

How many times have we thought we had a handle on a situation only to realize later, much to our chagrin, we weren't seeing the whole picture? The big picture is hard to grasp and requires information from the past that we can use quickly to formulate our understanding. Most of us will choose the path of least resistance most of the time. It's faster, easier, and more comfortable to formulate a belief using existing vs. new information.

Furthermore, the mental process that leads to making conclusions is increasingly abstract. Being able to jump a few steps and go from observation to action is a lot more appealing than taking what Chris Argyris has coined as the ladder of inference. (See a further discussion of this in chapter three, "Start with Yourself: How to Free Your Inner FROG.") The ladder has many steps:

> *observing data* ➡ *filtering data* ➡ *adding meaning to data* ➡
> *making an assumption* ➡ *drawing a conclusion* ➡ *updating our beliefs*
> ➡ *taking action.*

Ever wonder why we find it hard to recall when we first began to believe something is true? Probably because we failed to take all the steps of the ladder and just jumped in to action. It may also be it never occurred to us to question that truth at all.

Does the following story resonate with you at all?

A working team that was very close always took their lunch breaks together. A new member, Suzan, was hired and ate her first lunch break on her own reading a book. A few months later, Bryna was added to the team and sat with everyone else for lunch. She inquired why Suzan was sitting by herself, to which they replied, "She likes it that way."

Just before break was over, Bryna approached Suzan and said, "I noticed you sit by yourself at lunch, and if that's how you need to decompress that's absolutely fine. I just want you to know that the team is very friendly and if you want to join us tomorrow, you're most welcome."

Suzan burst into tears and said she had waited six months for somebody to invite her.

The team assumed Suzan wanted to eat by herself, not that she was waiting for an invitation. She assumed her colleagues didn't want her to join them or they would have asked her. It took an outgoing new member with fresh eyes to see past all the assumptions.

How to Explore Beliefs and Assumptions

We can push the pause button on our beliefs and assumptions, whether through self-reflection or in group dialogue, by asking:

- *What are the observable data behind that statement?*
- *What do we agree the data are?*
- *Can we run through the reasoning?*
- *How did we get from those data to these assumptions?*
- *When this was said/done ("your inference"), did it mean ("my interpretation of it")? If not, what else could it mean?*

Given that, rightly or wrongly, our experiences colour our assumptions and beliefs, a good way to overcome the roadblock of untrue assumptions is to make assumptions transparent in the moment so they don't build into a "clever story." Another way is to probe whether past assumptions are replicating themselves in the present. If we do not examine our assumptions, we will build and build on them, making "leaps of abstraction." Imagine framing and bricking a house before ensuring the foundation was watertight. How easy will it be to fix a foundation problem *later*? Not very. And it will cost you more in money, headaches, and attention.

This is the ideal place to practice the paradigm shift in which we make positive hypotheses and presuppositions. As discussed in chapter one, this requires us to listen to, build on, and select from what people are saying and what we can observe in our environment. This enables us to attend to talents, passions, and virtues rather than deficits, flaws, and disconnects.

Helping Lana, #4

Lana presented her new quality-management strategy to the leadership team and noticed some colleagues spent the whole time looking at their laptops. She floundered as she became frustrated that people were not listening to what took months of evenings and weekends to pull together. She assumed this was further evidence of what she already felt – that her colleagues didn't think what she did was important.

So she cut her presentation short, deciding then and there she would just report on her own programs next time rather than trying to support the whole organization.

As Lana's coach, mentor, or close friend, how would you help her debunk which data she selected, the meaning she added, the assumptions she made, the conclusions she drew, the beliefs the data reinforced, and the actions she took? How would you then help her to listen, build, and select data differently to come up with the most helpful belief system to fuel further action?

Strategies to Overcome Untrue Assumptions

The strategies below enable individuals and teams to look for the evidence behind their "truths." Ultimately, they help avoid the reflective loop that happens when we select the closest-fitting assumptions, in turn improving relationships and aligning our actions to reality. The strategies follow the listen, build, select approach. As we have explored throughout the book, recognition provides much-needed insulation to relationships, providing positive feedback and sheltering against untrue assumptions. Recognition shifts assumptions so they begin from a positive, factual place. These strategies are most easily leveraged when recognition is a solid foundation to culture and relationships.

- Evaluate your "truths," understanding that people are not black and white. When you find yourself believing staunchly in a "truth" that people's behaviours are simple to figure out, remember that what *you* do is made up of a very complex web of experiences, emotions, and reasons. It's important for you to be willing to suspect your "truth" just long enough to test it for other possibilities, particularly if this truth is not serving you or others well (e.g., it is making you feel frustrated or resentful). Through that testing, those truths you hold dear can be made visible to others as you are more explicit about them and advocate for them

- Inquire about others' truths and the thinking and reasoning behind them. Even if you don't believe in the same truth, knowing where the other person is coming from can help you agree to disagree or find suitable compromises

- Check out your beliefs. Just as you need to be mindful of your "truths," you also need to validate your beliefs before they become entrenched. Being compassionate with yourself when your beliefs do not hold water is part of being human

- Actively practice positive hypothesizing, which is the opposite of making negative assumptions. It is about immediately looking for and acknowledging the greatness in the person and their unique talents, passions, and virtues, judging the person by *that* cover

Guilt, Envy, and Other Unhelpful Emotions

Neuroscientists tell us that, due to evolution, we really have three brains. The ancient brain is small and the deepest part of our neo-cortex, our "reptilian" brain. It had many purposes, including supporting the ability to process a few very basic emotions that have allowed us to protect ourselves (i.e., fear) and procreate (i.e., lust). Two other layers – the mammalian "feeling" brain and then the primate "thinking" brain – evolved over time, allowing us, among other things, to experience much more complex emotions and meaning making. Perhaps this is why emotional intelligence – being able to read our own and others' emotions and respond appropriately – differentiates people who are able to excel in their lives and careers.

We suggest here that certain emotions are not quite as useful as the rest of the package. Examples include guilt, envy, and jealousy, which deplete our energy rather than build it up. They are often based on false assumptions and biased truths (as we've just discussed). They make us externally focused rather than internally resourceful. The more we see ourselves as having control over our situations (an internal locus of control), the more likely we are to look for opportunities and solutions rather than blame others or circumstances for something that's not working for us.

What if you thought of your emotions as tools to serve you? What if your policy were to check in every so often for whether an emotion was helping or hindering? Would you use a knife to eat yogurt or a spoon to cut bread? Of course not. *Emotions are our tools as social beings. We need to use them to interpret situations accurately, whether they are from the external world or created by ourselves, and debunk what is unhelpful.*

How Useful Are Emotions?

Think of an important relationship that is currently strained.
- *What emotions arise when you think of that person?*
- *Of these emotions, which one is the most intense?*
- *Currently, when does this emotion show up most strongly? When is it fully activated?*
- *How useful is this emotion? Is it helpful? In what way(s) is it not?*
- *If you got up in the morning to find the unhelpful emotion had been replaced with one that was helpful, what might it be? What would be the first indication the emotion had changed? What would be different? How would abandoning this less resourceful emotion be helpful?*
- *How might this emotion be disguised as a great opportunity? What might that opportunity be?*
- *If there were no risks, what actions could be taken to maximize this emotion?*

How many times have we read an email one way, only to find out its sender meant something completely different? Not checking in with ourselves or others when problematic emotions come up is like not checking out the context of that email. The decision point is: Do we want to truly understand what is driving an emotion or do we want to stay with it (i.e., facilitate a clever story)?

Here's a true story of runaway emotions from an unchecked assumption.

One day Stephany sent an email to her good friend and colleague Tina, which read as follows:

> Who are you? I am looking for the referral policy to update today.
> Please send as soon as possible.
> Stephany

Tina was offended and angry at Stephany's disrespectful introduction in the email and assumed she was taking over the project. She didn't speak with her for six months. Eventually the director of the area had to get involved. In a meeting in the director's office, Stephany remained confused and perplexed at Tina's claims of an offensive email. When asked to review the email, Stephany read it out loud as, "*How are you...*" not even seeing that "how" was actually typed "who."

Yes, a simple typo had ignited intense emotions leading to six months of hurt and missed opportunities to collaborate.

See how easily this can happen? Can you see yourself in this story?

We wouldn't want our new car to be delivered straight from the assembly line before it was checked over, so why would we let some of our most important relationships – those with our family, close co-workers, and even ourselves – go unchecked? Thinking back to what we just learned about assumptions, we know we're less likely to check false assumptions when we're in the grip of unhealthy or overwhelming emotions. *Checking the data and meaning that triggered an emotion can help us defuse the emotion so we can shift to feelings that can serve us better.*

The key first step, as we discussed in an earlier section on the inner critic, is to learn to recognize these emotions as a sign that something requires attention. The next step is to check in and reflect on the emotions. The longer we leave things, the harder it is for us to repair the relationship and other social systems. We're tempted to think of the broken relationship as being like a car that would cost more to fix than had we had budgeted for regular maintenance. We're likely to cut our losses and abandon the relationship in the social scrapyard. Unfortunately, others are impacted by which of our relationships are in good repair; part of our motivation to check our beliefs can be trying to prevent having a negative impact on others.

Helping Lana, #5

Lana's organization just finished updating all its policies, with the assistance of some staff and colleagues who offered to help. Lana was impressed by the record time in which they did this, as well as by how involving experienced staff made the policies more reflective of actual practice. The only damper was getting pulled in to heated exchanges between two people with hurt feelings and misinterpretations. Lana was the Director in the story we just described.

After she helped the two staff members to resolve their conflict, Lana spoke with her colleague, the head of HR, about how she could recognize the effort people had put in. She was at a loss as to how to recognize them all; she felt she had wasted a lot of time resolving a simple misunderstanding.

Staying with the belief everyone had greatness, Lana's colleague asked her if these individuals added any value whatsoever. Lana wrestled with the idea.

When Lana's colleague asked her if she thought all her staff felt valued for their wisdom and efforts, she admitted that she doubted it. "If anything," she said, "they have a reputation of being troublemakers. But I'm beginning to see they were actually really passionate people, and when I supported them, they became solution builders."

How might these reflections shift Lana's emotions? How could she capitalize on them in her efforts to recognize staff?

Strategies to Overcome Unhelpful Emotions

- One of the single most effective strategies for cutting through negative emotion and testing the opportunity to have an improved relationship with someone is to recognize something that *is* working. It may require digging really, really deep, but every person has greatness deserving of acknowledgement. Recognizing others face-to-face or when they aren't present (i.e., resource gossiping) can chip away at the unhealthy emotions. Retrace your story to see if a victim, villain, or helpless story is fuelling the emotions. If so, follow the steps outlined above and retrace your path to determine alternative stories and experience other emotions associated with them

- In situations where you feel you have little control, refocus on what you do have control over. You *always* have control over how you choose to react. How you feel is tied to how you behave. Shifting your thinking from what you don't have control over to what you do will likely shift your emotions to more helpful and resourceful ones

Fear of Conflict

Having trained and worked in therapeutic fields, we have become accustomed to helping people work through conflicts. As we've just discussed, it's important to work through conflicts as early as possible so negative emotions do not build up, making it more and more difficult to deal with them. Unfortunately, many of us hold many conflict-avoidance beliefs, sometimes from childhood. Ever hear expressions like *"Let sleeping dogs lie"* and *"Don't rock the boat"*? They come from the belief it's better to let things smooth over on their own over time than address them directly. Sometimes this works, but often it does not, for many reasons, including:

- One person may not realize there is a problem
- A situation can be interpreted as part of a bigger pattern of behaviour
- Power imbalances (perceived or real) can lead to relationship imbalance
- Other unhealthy strategies, such as speaking negatively about people behind their back (i.e., gossip), may be opted for instead
- The conflict can be based on data and beliefs that were false to begin with

Challenging Our "Truths" About Conflict

Most of us, when we hear the word "conflict," go to a very negative place, envisioning a battle or a war. Really, though, conflicts are often merely disagreements or differences of opinion. If we believed this:

- How might we engage in conversation differently?
- How might challenging our "truth" that conflict is bad enable us to consider how it might actually help us and strengthen our relationships?
- How might we be creative and produce out-of-the-box thinking and solutions?
- How might our new focus deepen our relationships? How might it help us understand ourselves and our needs better?
- How might the experience build our confidence?

We're not suggesting we should fuel conflict every time we disagree. There are many reasons to let something go, such as that an issue is not important to us or we don't have a relationship with someone (e.g., why bother to confront a stranger who cuts in line at the grocery store?). But it is also possible we choose to let something go as not a big deal when it actually triggered an unhealthy emotion about ourselves or the other person (e.g., our colleague makes a passing comment that offends us). The things we let go can build up over time, fostering negative and unhealthy emotions about people and situations. In other words, it's a balancing act.

Thomas and Kilmann developed a framework we sometimes use with clients outlining the five possible approaches we can take in a conflict situation:

1. Avoidance: low in assertiveness and low in cooperativeness.

2. Accommodating: low in assertiveness and high in cooperativeness.

3. Compromising: mild in assertiveness and mild in cooperativeness.

4. Competing: high in assertiveness and low in cooperativeness.

5. Collaborating: high in assertiveness and high in cooperativeness.

Research shows most people report using the less assertive styles of avoidance and accommodation the most.

People may avoid conflicts because they think it will benefit relationships, but avoidance can actually weaken them, as we learned in Tina and Stephany's story about the misunderstood email. Think of a time when you learned days or even months later that someone was upset about something you said or did and you were none the wiser, perhaps replying, *"I wish you had said something at the time."* If your friend had mentioned it, you could have cleared the air, explained what you meant, shared you didn't mean to cause upset, and figured out the best next step together.

Greatness requires both assertion and cooperation, which may mean you have to take a risk to get past an assumption. *Even in the moment of conflict, looking for the common ground right away and remembering the situation is between the two of you rather than inside either one of you will enable depersonalization and issue resolution.*

As we have noted in other parts of this chapter, recognition greases the wheels of healthy conflict. Or, to put it the way Stephen Covey does, when we take the opportunity to recognize someone when times are good, we make deposits into their "emotional bank account." A compliment or acknowledgement is a positive social gesture; if we need to disagree with someone, we want to be sure we have contributed to their emotional bank account first as they may see the conflict, at least at first, as a withdrawal. When conflicts are resolved properly, the balance of the emotional bank account will inevitably increase. The outcome of working through a conflict is greater respect for, and deeper understanding of, one another.

Strategies for Healthy Conflict

To get to a place where we believe conflict can assist our relationships rather than hinder them, we need to experiment. Here are a variety of ways to explore your own perceptions about conflict and methods you can try for the healthy resolution of issues.

- Reflect using the thoughts under "Challenging Our 'Truths' About Conflict" above
- Think of a conflict you feel you managed well. What worked?

- Think of a conflict situation you are currently experiencing. What is your default strategy? Consider all the conflict strategies to determine which may be most appropriate. What might you try differently if your default does not match the strategy that could be most helpful?

- Plan a productive opener to the conflict. A "harsh start-up" is one of the surest ways to ensure the conflict will be unproductive and lead to further hard feelings. No matter how strong the emotions are and how justified you may feel in having them, starting a conversation keyed up will only escalate the negativity, placing the two of you in opposing camps instead of a shared space

- Honour the other person's dignity and show respect throughout. Avoid sarcasm, blame, and other disrespectful behaviours at all costs, and apologize if you catch yourself using them

- Practice Stephen Covey's principle of *"seek first to understand, then to be understood."* It works because the goodwill and collaboration builds momentum to finding a solution together by believing common ground can be reached

- Recognize and genuinely acknowledge what greatness lies in the other person. A person who feels understood is less likely to be defensive. When you notice greatness during a conflict, the acknowledgement is all the more powerful as it demonstrates you are truly invested in improving the relationship; you build respect when you listen deeply during a challenging conversation to see greatness and share it

Avoidance of Challenging Conversations

If we avoid conflict, we reject the medium of challenging conversations. If our truth is, *"Conflict is bad,"* we may not have practiced and built up the skills for having challenging conversations and may lack the confidence to try them.

It may seem counterintuitive that healthier relationships are built from challenging one another through difficult conversations. Keep in mind, however, that these conversations are really about two things: (a) clearing the air so whatever issue or issues are resolved yield healthier relationships, and (b) making an investment in and respecting the other person to work through anything that could be a roadblock to mutual success. Clearing the air through challenging conversations allows both people to:

- Share their point of view
- Listen to understand
- Feel heard
- Discover values, beliefs, and interests that are shared and those that are unique
- Agree to disagree about some things
- Commit to shared agreements
- Shift unhealthy emotions to healthy ones

Challenging conversations, therefore, demonstrate an investment in the other person. That is why greater respect is gained as a result of challenging vs. abdicating our needs and views. The investment is in the form of:

- Both giving time and energy to the conversation (for many, time is a more valued commodity and in shorter supply than money)
- Demonstrating a willingness to be vulnerable in a variety of ways, including getting uncomfortable, admitting there may be another way to look at a situation, and sharing "power" in the conversation
- Hoping there is a future for the relationship
- Asking questions rather than telling, dominating the conversation, or trying to sell the other person on one point of view
- Using a neutral or caring tone and words instead of contemptuous or sarcastic ones
- Making statements that acknowledge greatness even when one or both of you in the conversation do not feel your greatness is shining through

---

Planning for a Challenging Conversation

Think of someone you are having difficulty with. Reflect on these questions:

1. The Intention:
- What needs to be achieved in the conversation?
- How can you both leave the conversation better off than before it started?
- What will be the benefit for you?
- What is a realistic goal for what success will look like in this conversation?

---

2. *Influence:*

- *What might the other person want to achieve from the conversation?*
- *What will be the benefit for that person?*
- *What does the person value most?*
- *What is easy to respect and value in the person?*
- *How could this be acknowledged?*

3. *Implement:*

- *Where and when can this conversation happen in order to set the right tone?*
- *What is the one thing you want this person to do differently?*
- *What repair attempts could you use if the conversation begins to go off the rails?*
- *What is this person doing that you really like?*
- *What talents, passions, and virtues could you acknowledge in the other person during the conversation?*

Planning challenging conversations is advisable for anyone, especially those who are used to avoiding them. How that preparation happens is a matter of preference. Introverts get their energy from within, so they may prefer to write down some thoughts or practice with a close friend. Extroverts, who get their energy from others, may prefer to practice a few versions from start to finish out loud, alone or with friends. However, it is not advisable for anyone to practice with people who are involved in the situation as this may degenerate into gossiping.

Helping Lana, #7

Lana has decided she is ready to have the conversation with her boss about what is not working in the structure of her job and her feeling that she is not recognized. She realizes she has had a victim story and she is no longer willing to accept it. Despite her decision, Lana is apprehensive and doesn't know where to start.

How could she prepare? What would be a reasonable expectation or goal for this first conversation? What would success look like? How could Lana celebrate what works? How could she learn from what doesn't?

Challenging Conversation Framework

We have created a challenging conversation framework that would help Lana, based on the insight of experts in this field such as M. B. Stanier, R. Fisher, and W. Ury, and the authors of the Crucial Conversations series, as well as scholars from the solution-focused world.

1. Start with the Facts	2. Express Your Emotions
List the objective, inarguable truth. Detail what actually happened.	Explain how the situation made you feel. Include all relevant emotions.
3. Check Your Assumptions	**4. Establish Your Goal**
Share your interpretations and judgements of what happened. What do you think about yourself, the other person, and the situation as a whole?	State your goal clearly. Commit to one small action yourself.

Moving through these steps sequentially allows for a paced conversation, one that goes deep enough to address the facts, feelings, and beliefs attached to the conflict while reducing the likelihood that defensiveness will derail it.

Dealing with Cold Feet

If you're getting cold feet about having a challenging conversation, reflect on the following questions. It may just heat them up enough for you to give it a try.

- *What is the worst that can happen?*
- *What is the best that can happen?*
- *What is the difference between the worst and the best? How could that gap be closed even just a little?*

Strategies for Effective Challenging Conversations

They say nothing worth doing comes without effort. Much of what allows us to grow is achieved only when we push ourselves past our comfort zone. Here are some strategies to help you become more comfortable with and effective in having challenging conversations.

- Plan your challenging conversation until you consistently feel comfortable walking in to them cold. Use the box above, "Planning for a Challenging Conversation," to help with this

- Early in the conversation, establish good intentions by indicating the goal you have for it is not for your personal gain but is of shared value

- Give the other person the A. Believe the other person is respectful and resourceful enough for a good outcome. Consistently treat the other person as a good, ethical, competent person with no ill intent

- Ask for help addressing the issue; elicit ideas for how it can be resolved and the relationship improved. Ask *"What else?"* so as many ideas can be generated as possible and the root of the issue is surfaced

- Get curious with ideas (e.g., *"I am wondering if..."* *"Can you tell me more about..."*). Even when an option is selected, explore together next steps and the plan to successfully execute it. *"How will we both know it was successful?"* *"What should the contingency plan be if something doesn't go according to plan?"*

- Acknowledge greatness whenever it shows up. Point out the things most valued in the other person and why the relationship is important

- If the conflict is not resolved satisfactorily, consider getting assistance from a neutral party with the skills to mediate. It could be a supervisor, organizational development professional, human resources consultant, ombudsperson, mediator, or even a neutral colleague not directly involved

---

Closing Reflection
Dealing with Roadblocks
- *What have you learned about the various roadblocks mentioned in this chapter?*
- *What do you now recognize about your circle of influence? How has that shifted the way you will think of roadblocks in the future?*
- *What do you now realize is blocking others you work with closely? How could recognizing their greatness help them with their roadblock?*
- *What greatness do you want to recognize in yourself at this moment that will help support your resiliency in facing roadblocks in the future?*
- *How might it assist you in dealing with current and future roadblocks to leverage more of the talents, passions, and virtues you already have?*

Inspiration for **Action**

Conflict is nothing more than an opportunity for greater growth and a deeper connection.

—Robin Sharma

People are trying to collaborate all the time…just not each other's way.

—Jim Duval

Every human being is trying to say something to others. Trying to cry out I am alive, notice me! Speak to me! Confirm that I am important, that I matter!

—Marion D. Hanks

Whenever you're in conflict with someone, there is one factor that can make the difference between damaging your relationship and deepening it. That factor is attitude.

—William James

Negative emotions like loneliness, envy, and guilt have an important role to play in a happy life; they're big, flashing signs that something needs to change.

—Gretchen Rubin

You have to change something, not someone.

—Mark McKergow

Conclusion

The Thirty-Day Recognition Challenge

We're curious where you are in this phase of your journey – about what drove you to pick up and read this book – and what you have discovered and planned for yourself. Recognizing greatness, after all, is an ongoing process; it's not over just because you've reached these final pages.

Take a moment to acknowledge where you are already. Think back to the best hopes you had when you started reading.

- *On a scale of 10 to 1, with 10 standing for obtaining all the knowledge and insight in this book and 1 being the opposite of that, where are you now?*
- *What are you clearer about? Why is this important to you?*
- *What strategies have you tried that worked? What strategies did not work as well as you hoped? What did you learn from this?*
- *What does your recognizing-greatness intention look like right now?*
- *How have you attempted to ritualize recognition of greatness in your work or personal life?*
- *What impact has recognition had on others? What difference did it make when you focused on greatness over deficits? To what extent have you detected the boomerang effect?*

Many of our clients by this point in their work with us choose to elevate their FROG intention. One strategy we would like to offer you is the Thirty-Day Recognition Challenge. If you have not done so already, we encourage you to recognize your own and others' talents, passions, and virtues at least once every day for thirty days. As discussed in chapter two, changing a habit, while not easy, is doable. Given that it takes at least twenty-one days of consistently engaging in a new activity to form a habit, we suggest a target of one month to help you ensure this intention is a success.

You already know how most people say they prefer to be recognized – with a verbal thank you, a private word of praise, or a handwritten thank-you note – and we have explored evolving ways of recognizing people, through social media, organizational events, and conversations with people about how they like to be recognized. We have also included a list in Appendix A of over eighty specific ways to recognize others' greatness. We know you will easily add to that list. What ways will you select to effortlessly and authentically recognize yourself and others every day?

A FROG Brain Teaser
Five frogs were on a ledge. One decided to jump. How many remain?
Five. Just because one of them decided to jump doesn't mean he acted.

We encourage you to revisit this book any time you find seeing your own greatness a challenge, or when you're struggling with recognition in the groups or teams you associate with regularly. New insights and inspirations can come when you read with fresh eyes.

We look forward to hearing how you have successfully spread FROG in your life and created a positive ripple effect.

Closing Reflection
- *What area of recognition that we have not yet explored would you like to research further?*
- *What role would you like greatness to play in your life? How will you know it is working for you?*
- *What question do you need to ask yourself right now?*
- *Suppose it is six months from now. What will people notice that is different about you? How will you recognize yourself differently? How will you recognize others differently?*
- *What will you have realized was working all along, which you then recommitted to?*
- *What is your next step?*

Appendix A

80+ Ways to Recognize Greatness

1. Tell people exactly what you think they did well in the moment.
2. Provide a thumbs-up after a presentation.
3. Make a public comment of praise.
4. Provide a private comment of praise.
5. Ask for their opinion on a problem (and act on it).
6. Affirm that they handled a difficult situation well.
7. Keep them "in the loop."
8. Trust them with sensitive information.
9. Text a note of recognition.
10. Email a thank-you note.
11. CC others on your thank-you note.
12. Give a genuine smile (that reaches your eyes).
13. Reflect how much you are seeing them grow (specifics, please).
14. Send a handwritten thank-you note.
15. Get others to join you in writing a thank-you card.
16. Write a small blurb (on them, the success of their project, an improvement they're trialing) for an internal newsletter.
17. Buy them a tea or coffee (especially if you remember what they take in it).

18. Make them a tea or coffee.

19. Give them a package of their favourite tea or coffee.

20. Give them a small token of something they like.

21. Attach a note of acknowledgement to the gift.

22. Praise them to someone else at work (even when they won't know you did so).

23. Praise them to someone else at work (when they can hear it).

24. Acknowledge what you value in them to their close family member or friend at a gathering.

25. Remind them of their talents, passions, and virtues when they doubt themselves.

26. Coach them through a problem or decision until they decide what they should do.

27. Give them your undivided attention when they need it.

28. Mentor them in a new skill.

29. Provide career advice in a solution-focused way ("*I am wondering…*")

30. Affirm you know their dreams or goals will become a reality.

31. Acknowledge something nice they did for someone else (pay it forward).

32. Give them more responsibility in a way they can grow.

33. Tell them specifically what you admire about or learned from them.

34. Let them take full credit for great work (even when you helped to make it successful).

35. Organize a work potluck in their honour (retirement, new job, work anniversary…).

36. Organize a social outing to celebrate a milestone.

37. Order pizza for a team celebration.

38. Acknowledge them in your speech at a party in your honour.

39. Offer to help when you see they are tired or overwhelmed.

40. Tell them, when they're having a bad day, that you appreciate how they give 100% when they can.

41. Forward an inspirational quote (noting why it reminded you of them).

42. Suggest they should be included on an important project.

43. Offer to present at a conference together.

44. Nominate them for an award at work.

45. Nominate them for an award in their profession.

46. Nominate them for an award in their community.

47. Nominate them for a scholarship or bursary.

48. Tell them about a funding opportunity (and why you feel they are worth every penny).

49. Take them as your guest to a networking event.

50. Introduce them to someone who could help their career.

51. Make e-introductions to influential people who could open doors for them.

52. Recommend them to the nominations committee of a board they would like to join.

53. Mentor them when they join a new organization or board.

54. Recommend them for a job (to your employer or someone you know who's hiring).

55. Write a letter of recommendation.

56. Be a reference.

57. Give them a letter of recommendation before they ask.

58. Give them a job tip.

59. Forward information to them on courses, conferences, or certificate programs you think they'd do well in and tell them why.

60. Acknowledge their contributions in a publication you wrote.

61. Post a recommendation to LinkedIn.

62. Recommend them for specific skills on LinkedIn.

63. Like their LinkedIn updates.

64. Respond to a LinkedIn article by noting how they emulate the article's topic.

65. Favourite one of their LinkedIn articles.

66. Introduce them to a good social media contact.

67. Personalize a social media congratulation regarding work milestones.

68. Retweet one of their tweets.

69. Favourite one of their tweets.

70. Tweet a picture of them doing something great.

71. Tweet something you heard them say (quote them to fame).

72. Blog something you heard them say.

73. Blog about something you learned from them or why they inspire you.

74. Invite them to be a guest blogger.

75. Write an acknowledging introduction to their guest blog.

76. Forward their blog post.

77. Like a Facebook update.

78. Comment on their Facebook update.

79. Post a note of praise on a Facebook wall.

80. Like a company Facebook page.

81. Share a picture of someone deserving recognition on Facebook.

82. Participate in a recognition planning committee.

83. Give a small token of recognition (e.g., little squashy frog) and explain why they deserve it.

84. Make up a funny poem in their honour.

85. Share an acknowledging story about them at a team event.

86. Cover their role so they can take a much-deserved break.

Appendix B

FAQs

How can I recognize people when I have no budget?

Many leaders struggle to find ways to recognize people on limited budgets, and always dipping in to their own pocket can start to add up. Appendix A above lists over 80 ways to recognize people. Most of them are free. Giving of your time is often more appreciated than a token gift.

How can I fairly recognize people?

Sometimes people worry about being perceived as playing favourites. Remember, if your intention is solid, you're on the right track. You can't control how people perceive a gesture, but you can control the motivation behind it. If you endeavour to "catch people in greatness," you'll end up recognizing a range of people because you'll notice the variety of greatness all around you.

We think it's also important to keep in mind that recognition is everyone's job, not just the leader's. Professionals should be self-aware and self-reflective enough to recognize when they are surpassing their skills and abilities and should acknowledge the greatness of their peers. In other words, the role of the leader is to foster a recognition culture. If it's not just up to you, then recognition becomes more sustainable and self-reinforcing. It becomes less about who and how you recognize people and more about how you enable people to honour their own greatness and that of their peers.

Trust the team will be able to catch those moments of greatness. After all, they're with one another way more hours than you as a leader are. Wouldn't it be cool if it became your job to acknowledge the recognition happening among team members? The question of fairness would begin to disappear if people felt they were being recognized by their peers and that you valued this.

How do I recognize people who are not performing well?

Everyone does something that is their form of greatness. We're not saying it's always obvious or even easy to find that thing, but often it is tied to something the individual values most. As soon as you begin noticing what the person is doing *right* vs. pointing out what is wrong, he or she will be more motivated to do things that fit expectations. Sometimes we need to look deep to find something we respect and value in the other person. This will help in establishing trust. Once trust is built, it's much easier to ask people what they feel they excel at and what they would like to improve.

How do I recognize people when I have over a hundred direct reports?

When this many people report to you, it's nearly impossible to recognize everyone on a regular enough basis that people would say, *"Boy, my boss has this recognition thing down to a science!"* That's not to say you won't make this part of your daily work. It's simply an acknowledgement that trying to recognize every single person will make you think of yourself as letting your team down rather than noticing the greatness of what you *are* doing. Acknowledge to yourself when you do take the time to recognize people. Spread acknowledgement around. You'll get to everyone if you're generous with your recognition and realize that everyone's greatness will look a little different.

We strongly suggest you focus your energy on building a culture where recognition is a regular, healthy, and fluid part of the work environment. Teach resource gossiping and practice it. When there is a conflict, publicly acknowledge the greatness in both parties and express confidence that their greatness will enable a solution to be found. Ask about what is working before pointing out what is wrong. Empower those who are experts to make the suggestions rather than solving a problem for them if in fact it's perfectly within their role to address the issue. Leading FROG-style and creating a culture of FROG is one of the most important ways you can ensure everyone gets recognized, because recognition is no longer the job of just the leader.

How do I balance recognizing unpaid volunteers with recognizing paid staff?

Everyone has greatness, so the advice above applies to volunteers as well as staff. What does the team feel is the best way to recognize the greatness in volunteers (as a collective or as individuals)? What support could you provide the team to help with this, and how can you contribute as a colleague? Again, it's not all up to you if you are fuelling a healthy recognition culture.

Why do I need to recognize people – isn't getting a paycheque enough?

As we discussed right at the beginning of this book, people vote with their feet when they don't feel valued, and in the talent shortage of today, we just can't afford for that to happen. Like it or not, a bigger motivator for people than money is recognition. Why? People are human beings, and it's the humanity of recognition that connects them to one another and their organization. More and more, people want to belong to something. Work can feel like a community or a jail sentence (or something in between). In which scenario are you likely get the best from people: when they feel they can contribute with purpose or when they show up out of obligation?

I don't get recognized. Why should I recognize others?

The surest way to be recognized is to recognize the greatness in others. It's pretty hard for us to be annoyed, angry, or apathetic with someone who sees our talents, passions, and virtues, expresses an appreciation for them, and finds ways to draw them out of us. We also suggest you reflect on the exercises in chapter three, "Start with Yourself: How to Free Your Inner FROG." How are you focused on self-recognition? If you're grounded in your own greatness and have found ways to live it in meaningful ways, others' recognition of you naturally becomes less important. It is ironic, isn't it?

I've tried recognizing people and they don't appreciate it. Why bother?

Rome wasn't built in a day, and neither was a team's ecosystem destroyed in one. It takes seven years to build a culture, and every day we take small steps forward. Focus on the steps, on the small markers of progress along the way, and celebrate them. We suspect you'll be better able to see the small examples of where recognition is happening rather than attending to all the evidence it is not present. While you're at it, do a self-recognition check-in. Have you recognized yourself lately? Turn recognition inwards. You always have control over that!

I have only so much time in my day. How do I balance recognition along with all the other things I need to do?

In its simplest form, recognizing greatness happens in the moment. Come to work prepared to recognize greatness when you see it. We always carry little squishy frogs, frog charms, and recognition cards in our pockets and purses. That way we can recognize someone in the moment as soon as we witness it. What is your easy and quick method?

We agree you don't have time to plan a huge celebration every day or go shopping for the perfect gift. Good thing that's not how employees most want to be recognized, isn't it?

Is recognition just the leader's job?

Glad you asked! We suggest you review sections of the book where we talk about this, but in the meantime, note that, while people say they most want to be recognized by their direct supervisor, the strongest cultures we have witnessed are those where everyone sees it as their role to recognize greatness – in clients, colleagues, subordinates, superiors – in creative and personal ways every day. How would you feel more energized at the end of the day, if your boss shared specifically how she thought you did a good job or a client, colleague, or work friend shared how much they valued your greatness? Maybe you would say both (we don't blame you).

Should I recognize people when it's not valued in my organization?

Haven't some of the most powerful and transformational changes happened in this world at a grassroots level? Why not start where you have control – with those you work with, interact with, and care about – and see where it takes you? *Recognition feeds souls, yours included.* And anyway, if you face backlash for recognizing greatness, do you really want to work there? Living your greatness is how you will live with purpose and passion. Don't give your power over to any force willing to stifle it. Be yourself. Be great.

Appendix C

Metrics@Work

Dr. John Yardley started Metrics@Work Inc. as the Workplace Health Research Laboratory (WHRL) at Brock University, St. Catharines, Ontario, where it operated from 1999 to 2007. In September 2007, Metrics@Work was formally incorporated as an applied research company focusing on human resource management.

Metrics@Work (also known as WHRL) has worked with organizations ranging in size from 50 employees to over 70,000 employees (the majority of organizations being in the range of 250 to 5,000 employees), focusing on the collection, analysis, reporting, and actioning of employee, customer, and organizational data. Metrics@Work has the most working experience in the sectors of Education, Healthcare, Government (especially Municipal / City), Finance, and Technology. It has worked in almost all provinces and territories of Canada and has several clients with international sites and work groups, which has necessitated surveys in multiple languages.

Since 1999, the organization has created well over 400 employee surveys, as well as numerous customer, volunteer, and physician surveys with a database that exceeds 300,000 respondents. The organization's analytical systems are based on sound theory and constructed to meet high standards of validity and reliability, and are designed to provide leading edge, practical recommendations to promote better people management practices and working relationships.

Metrics@Work focuses on five major elements:

1. Organizational Surveying:

   a. Employee or staff engagement surveys, including pulse surveys
   b. Customers / clients / patients

c. Volunteers

d. 360-degree feedback

e. Board Governance

2. Data Mining: In-depth analyses of any form of empirical data, with approaches to the thematic analyses of qualitative data, e.g., survey open commentary, focus group information.

3. Intra-Organizational Presentations and Workshops with two primary foci:

   a. Presentations of organizational and database information to organizational groups, e.g., Senior Management, Management, Staff, Boards.

   b. Workshops related to strategic topics (e.g., Harassment in the Workplace, Leadership Development, Change Management).

4. Organizational Assessments: Primarily organizational development and strategic planning with a focus on Human Resource Management.

5. Speaking and Training and Development Workshops: these are conducted for the most part by Dr. Yardley and include the topics of, leadership, team development, change management, incivility, and harassment.

Contact information:
www.metricsatwork.com
1-800-726-4082
info@metricsatwork.com

Bibliography

Adams, M. (2009). *Change Your Questions, Change Your Life: 10 Powerful Tools for Life and Work*. 2nd ed. San Francisco: Berrett-Koehler.

Argyris, C. (1993). *Knowledge for Action: A Guide to Overcoming Barriers to Organizational Change*. San Francisco: Jossey-Bass.

———. (1993). *On Organizational Learning*. Cambridge, MA: Blackwell.

Bannink, F. (2014). *Post Traumatic Success: Positive Psychology & Solution-Focused Strategies to Help Clients Survive & Thrive*. New York: W.W. Norton.

———. (2010). *Solution-Focused Conflict Management*. Cambridge, MA: Hogrefe.

Baranowsky, A. B., & Gentry, J. E. (1997). *Compassion Fatigue Resiliency and Recovery: The Accelerated Recovery Program for Compassion Fatigue*. <http://www.tir.org/research_pub/research/compassion_fatigue.html>.

Bersin, J., Agarwal, D., Pelster, B., & Schwartz, J. (2015). *Global Human Capital Trends 2015: Leading in the New World*. Available at <http://www2.deloitte.com/us/en/pages/human-capital/articles/introduction-human-capital-trends.html>.

Bridges, W., with Bridges, S. (2009). *Managing Transitions: Making the Most of Change*. Philadelphia: Perseus Books.

Buckingham, M. (2007). *Go Put Your Strengths to Work: 6 Powerful Steps to Achieve Outstanding Performance*. New York: Free Press.

Buckingham, M., & Clifton, D. (2001). *Now, Discover Your Strengths: How to Develop Your Talents and Those of the People You Manage*. New York: Free Press.

———. (1999). *First, Break all the Rules: What the World's Greatest Managers Do Differently*. New York: Simon & Schuster.

Cavanagh, S. J. (1991). Conflict Management Style of Staff Nurses and Nurse Managers. *Journal of Advanced Nursing 16(10)*, 1254–60.

Chapman, G., & White, P. (2012). *The 5 Languages of Appreciation in the Workplace: Empowering Organizations by Encouraging People*. Chicago: Northfield.

Covey, S. R. (2008). *The Speed of Trust: The One Thing That Changes Everything*. New York: Simon & Schuster.

_____ . (2004). *The 7 Habits of Highly Effective People: Powerful Lessons in Personal Change*. New York: Simon & Schuster.

De Jong, P., & Berg, I. K. (2001). *Interviewing for Solutions*. 4th ed. Belmont, CA: Brooks/Cole.

Dolan, Y. M. (1991). *Resolving Sexual Abuse*. New York: W.W. Norton.

Duhigg, C. (2012). *The Power of Habit: Why We Do What We Do in Life and Business*. New York: Random House.

Figley, C. (1995). *Compassion Fatigue: Coping with Secondary Traumatic Stress Disorder in Those Who Treat the Traumatized*. New York: Routledge.

Fishbein, M., & Ajzen, I. (2010). *Predicting and Changing Behavior: The Reasoned Action Approach*. New York: Taylor & Francis.

Fisher R., & Ury, W. (2011). *Getting to Yes: Negotiating Agreement Without Giving In*. Toronto: Penguin.

Fiske, H. (2008). *Hope in Action: Solution-Focused Conversations About Suicide*. New York: Routledge.

Gostick, A., & Elton, C. (2010). *The Orange Revolution: How One Great Team Can Transform an Entire Organization*. New York: Free Press.

_____ . (2007). *The Carrot Principle: How the Best Managers Use Recognition to Engage Their People, Retain Talent, and Accelerate*. New York: Free Press.

Herk, N. A., Thompson, R. C., & Thomas, K. W. (2011). International Technical Brief for the Thomas-Kilmann Conflict Mode Instrument. *CPP White Paper*. Mountain View, CA: CPP, Inc.

Izzo, J. (2011). *Stepping Up: How Taking Responsibility Changes Everything*. San Francisco: Berrett-Koehler.

Jackson, P. Z., & McKergow, M. (2011). *The Solutions Focus: Making Coaching and Change Simple*. London: Nicholas Brealey International.

Knapp, L., Putnam, L. L., & Davis, L. J. (1988). Measuring Interpersonal Conflict in Organizations: Where Do We Go from Here? *Management Communications Quarterly 1(3)*, 414–29.

Kotter, J. P. (1996). *Leading Change*. Boston: Harvard Business School Press.

Kotter, J. P., & Cohen, D. S. (2002). *The Heart of Change: Real-Life Stories of How People Change Their Organizations*. Boston: Harvard Business School Press.

Kotter, J. P., & Rathgeber, H. (2006). *Our Iceberg Is Melting: Changing and Succeeding Under Any Conditions*. New York: St. Martin's Press.

Kress, S. (2012). *Learning in Thin Air*. Toronto: Oblio Press.

Lang, E. (2009). *The Frogs and Toads of North America: A Comprehensive Guide to Their Identification, Behavior, and Calls*. New York: Houghton, Mifflin, Harcourt.

Liker, J. K. (2004). *The Toyota Way: 14 Management Principles from the World's Greatest Manufacturer*. New York: McGraw-Hill.

Lundin, S., & Nelson, B. *Ubuntu! An Inspiring Story About an African Tradition of Teamwork and Collaboration*. New York: Random House.

Malinen, T., Cooper, S. J., & Thomas, F. N. Eds. *Masters of Narrative and Collaborative Therapies: The Voices of Andersen, Anderson, and White*. New York: Routledge.

Mehrabian, A. (1971). *Silent Messages: Implicit Communication of Emotions and Attitudes*. Wadsworth, CA: Belmont.

Nelson, B. (2012). *1501 Ways to Reward Employees*. New York: Workman.

_____. (2005). *1001 Ways to Reward Employees*. New York: Workman.

Nelson, B., & Spitzer, D. (2003). *The Complete Guide: The 1001 Rewards & Recognition Fieldbook*. New York: Workman.

Nelson, T. (2010). *Doing Something Different: Solution-Focused Brief Therapy Practices*. New York: Routledge.

_____. (2005). *Education and Training in Solution-Focused Brief Therapy*. New York: Routledge.

Patterson, K., Grenny, J., Maxfield, D., McMillan, R., & Switzler, A. (2008). *Influencer: The Power to Change Anything*. New York: McGraw-Hill.

Patterson, K., Grenny, J., McMillan, R., & Switzler, A. (2008). *Crucial Confrontations: Tools for Resolving Broken Promises, Violated Expectations, and Bad Behavior*. New York: McGraw-Hill.

Patterson, K., Grenny, J., McMillan, R., & Switzler, A. (2004). *Crucial Conversations: Tools for Talking When Stakes Are High*. New York: McGraw-Hill.

Pearlman, L. A, Saakvitne, K. W. (1995). *Trauma and the Therapist: Countertransference and Vicarious Traumatization in Psychotherapy with Incest Survivors*. New York: W.W. Norton.

Senge, P. (2006). *The Fifth Discipline: The Art & Practice of the Learning Organization*. New York: Doubleday.

Senge, P., Kleiner, A., Roberts, C., Ross, R., & Smith, B. (1994). *The Fifth Discipline Fieldbook: Strategies and Tools for Building a Learning Organization*. New York: Crown Business.

Shaked, D. (2013). *Strength-Based Lean Six Sigma: Building Positive and Engaging Business Improvement*. Philadelphia: Kogan Page.

Sharma, R. (2007). *The Greatness Guide*. Book 2. Toronto: HarperCollins.

Sinek, S. (2009). *Start with Why: How Great Leaders Inspire Everyone to Take Action*. New York: Penguin.

Stone, D., Patton, D., & Heen, S. (2010). *Difficult Conversations: How to Discuss What Matters Most*. New York: Penguin.

Stubblefield, A. (2004). *The Baptist Health Care Journey to Excellence: Creating a Culture That WOWs!* Hoboken, NJ: John Wiley & Sons.

Szabó, P. & Berg, I. K. (2005). *Brief Coaching for Lasting Solutions*. New York: W.W. Norton.

Szabó, P., Meier, D., & Dierolf, K. (2009). *Coaching Plain & Simple: Solution-Focused Brief Coaching Essentials*. New York: W.W. Norton.

Thomas, K. W. (2006). Making Conflict Management a Strategic Advantage. *CPP White Paper*. <https://www.cpp.com/pdfs/conflict_whitepaper.pdf>.

Thomas, K., Fann Thomas, G., & Schaubht, N. (2008). Conflict Styles of Men and Women at Six Organizational Levels. *International Journal of Conflict Management, 19(2)*, 148–66.

Thomas, P. H. (2009). *Be Great: The Five Foundations of an Extraordinary Life in Business – and Beyond*. Mississauga, ON: John Wiley & Sons.

Young, S. (2009). *Solution-Focused Schools: Anti-Bullying and Beyond*. London: BT Press.

Warrell, M. (2013). *Stop Playing Safe: Rethink Risk, Unlock the Power of Communication, Achieve Outstanding Success*. Milton, Qld, Australia: John Wiley & Sons.

Womack, D. F. (1988). A Review of Conflict Instruments in Organizational Settings. *Management Communications Quarterly 1(3)*, 437–45.

Zander, B., & Zander, R. S. (2000). *The Art of Possibility: Transforming Professional & Personal Life*. New York: Penguin.

About the Authors

Sarah McVanel

With roots in humanistic psychology, Sarah uses the mediums of coaching, facilitation, and training to help individuals, teams, and organizations leverage their existing gifts and talents to reach their full potential. She has evolved her style through her training to be a human resources, organizational development, and coaching professional and through various specialist and leadership roles in the public sector.

Most recently Sarah left a senior leadership role to start her own business, Greatness Magnified, giving her more time to write, continue to grow her professional speaking career, and secretly study the greatness in her kids, Justin and Simonne, and husband, Mark.

Brenda Zalter-Minden

Brenda is the Principal and Founder of BZM Solutions, a business that helps organizations, teams, and individuals flourish utilizing a solution-focused approach. Her passion for this line of work grew throughout her ten-year employment in healthcare as an internal consultant. She has gained a wealth of experience over the last twenty-six years in various capacities. Her areas of specialization currently include leadership, management, team building, coaching, facilitating, and creating workshops.

Brenda has taught postgraduate students part-time for Toronto Advanced Professional Education (T.A.P.E), Faculty of Social Work, Continuing Education, affiliated with the University of Toronto, as well as for the Adler Learning Centre. She teaches solution-focused interventions on a variety of topics.

She had the privilege of being trained by both Insoo Kim Berg and Steve de Shazer, the founders of the solution-focused model. She has adapted their philosophy and has created FROG – Forever Recognize Others' Greatness™. This unique approach builds on strengths, inspires change, and empowers a continuous improvement culture for both management and staff.

At the same time, Brenda enjoys life to the fullest…one day at a time.

Notes

CPSIA information can be obtained
at www.ICGtesting.com
Printed in the USA
LVHW04s0330300518
578794LV00002B/2/P

9 781772 360257